YEGOR GAIDAR, ANATOLY CHUBAIS

Crossroads in Modern Russian History

Crossroads in Modern Russian History

By

Yegor Gaidar, Anatoly Chubais

Translated by Antonina W. Bouis

Duncker & Humblot · Berlin

Bibliografische Information der Deutschen Nationalbibliothek

Die Deutsche Nationalbibliothek verzeichnet diese Publikation in der Deutschen Nationalbibliografie; detaillierte bibliografische Daten sind im Internet über http://dnb.d-nb.de abrufbar.

First published in Russian by Egor Gaydar Foundation under the title „Razvilki Noveishey Istorii Rossii" by Yegor Gaidar and Anatoly Chubais.
This edition has been translated and published under licence from Antonina W. Bouis.

Druck: buchbücher.de gmbh, Birkach
Printed in Germany

Umschlagbild: Moskau, Luftaufnahme, © Pavel Burchenko – Fotolia.com

ISBN 978-3-428-14853-0 (Print)
ISBN 978-3-428-54853-8 (E-Book)
ISBN 978-3-428-84853-9 (Print & E-Book)

Gedruckt auf alterungsbeständigem (säurefreiem) Papier
entsprechend ISO 9706 ♾

Internet: http://www.duncker-humblot.de

Foreword

This is a small book about big historical issues by two great men. Apart from Boris Yeltsin, nobody has done more to the benefit of modern Russia than late Yegor Gaidar and Anatoly Chubais. Both have written several books about Russia's transition to a market economy, in which they were both strategists and executives, but this book has several advantages. The authors take on many of the big controversial issues of Russia's transition. They give their critics clear answers with ample statistical evidence and convincing arguments. For a supporter of a market economy, it is difficult to disagree with them. The brevity of this book has rendered it lucid and easy to read.

Gaidar and Chubais were the leaders of the Russian economic reforms. Regardless of their specific positions, they consulted each other closely before and after the reforms. While both were outstanding intellectuals, Gaidar was the foremost economic strategist and Chubais the preeminent executive who knew how to get anything done. I first met Chubais in September 1990 and Gaidar in June 1991. Already then, they were striking personalities. After you had met them, you knew that they were the leaders of the future and we kept in touch ever since. In June 1991, I took two Swedish colleagues to see Gaidar at his new Institute of Economic Policy. When we left, I told them that I thought Gaidar would be Russia's next prime minister. They looked at me with surprise, but they were all the more impressed when he was appointed in November 1991. Gaidar and Chubais and their team were simply superior to any competitors. It shows Yeltsin's greatness that he realized that.

In this book, Gaidar and Chubais discuss the big contentious issues of their government. I shall only illuminate a few of them. In his book *Collapse of an Empire*, Gaidar discussed in considerable detail the implosion of the Soviet Union. Here the authors concentrate on the main points, rendering them all the more evident. The key insight is that the Soviet Union collapsed in a profound and multifaceted fashion. The only responsible course of action was to separate the Soviet republics as fast and cleanly as possible. Yeltsin, Gaidar and Chubais all understood that, and Yeltsin and Gaidar effectuated it. The also comprehended the importance of maintaining the existing borders however odd they might have appeared.

They but few others realized that the alternative could all too easily have been a prolonged and bloody civil war as Yugoslavia went through in the 1990s because of a Serb desire to hold that untenable state together. This insight has gained new relevance with the recent wars in Georgia and Ukraine. Yeltsin's wise actions might still be undone.

Nobody understood better than Gaidar and Chubais that nature abhors vacuum. The old system had to be abandoned and a new one built as soon as possible. They realized the importance of speed. In hindsight, it appears rather absurd that they were accused of being "Bolsheviks" for their desire to solve vital national problems quickly. Why should people suffer for longer than necessary? Moreover, any delay would be exploited by the old communist elite to recover their hold on the state. As Estonian reformist Prime Minister Mart Laar put it: "To wait means to fail." The problem with Russia's reforms was not that they were too fast but too slow. Only in 1999 were they sufficiently complete to return Russia to economic growth. The tardiness of the Russian reforms, which Gaidar and Chubais opposed so vehemently, facilitated the return of so many members of the old regime to power and to transform that power into wealth. The rupture with the old system and elite should have been much sharper, as Gaidar and Chubais argued.

Gaidar's outstanding achievement was that he formulated, the "Gaidar program," a clear strategy for Russia's transition to a market economy. He did so in a frightfully difficult economic and political situation. It is easy to criticize a strategy because no strategy is perfect, but as Poland's great reformer Leszek Balcerowicz has pointed out: "A risky strategy is always better than a hopeless strategy." Worst of all is no strategy, which was characteristic of most of the Russian critics of radical market reform.

Chubais is the father of private enterprise in Russia. Without his ingenuity and skills, privatization could hardly have been possible. Chubais tried all kinds of different privatization schemes with a clear understanding that capitalism does require private enterprises. The book displays the accomplishments that arose with privatization. Without the loans-for-shares privatization in 1995 it is doubtful that the stellar recovery of the Russian oil industry would have been possible.

Gaidar and Chubais do not condone all the practices of private businessmen. They also depict their battles with Russia's big businessmen, notably in 1997, when they lost. Their ideal is a well-functioning competitive market economy with predominantly private enterprises and based on the rule of law.

Leadership matters especially in a transition between two systems when old institutions are on the vane and few new institutions have taken shape. Many countries transition from socialist economies to market economies, with varying success depending on preconditions and policy. Each successful reform country, however, had its heroes, its reform leaders.

A sobering thought is that if Yeltsin, Gaidar and Chubais had not been there, Russia might have ended up like a post-communist state economy, such as Belarus, Turkmenistan or Uzbekistan. The success of the market economy and privatization was never a given, and without these three true leaders, it might never have happened. Russians need to learn who their true heroes are. Therefore, this handy book by two of them is a nice and worthwhile read.

Anders Åslund

Advisor to the Russian government, 1991–94

Contents

Eyewitness to History

Yevgeny Yasin

What is this book's greatest plus? It explains in clear and simple terms the decisions taken in those fateful years, at which crossroads of history the need for such decisions occurred, and what limitations forced one action rather than another, even if the other was preferred by the authors. Let me stress a factor known to us all: the authors are not historians but the people who elaborated and made those fateful decisions and took full responsibility for them. It is a rare case in our history: they had all the qualities necessary to execute their lofty mission. In other cases, the majority of them, the most serious decisions with far-reaching consequences were made by people who had an extremely distorted idea of reality and were guided by dubious, often petty, and avaricious interests. Such decisions inevitably led the country onto marginal, if not dead-end, trajectories from which we had to return with losses.

The book is divided into chapters devoted to certain periods of our twentieth-century history, the shortest of which is just two years (1992–93), the one in which they worked. Chubais worked in government later as well, until March 1998, but that was already another time. Their main accomplishments belong to the period 1992–93. In no other period during that century was the scale of the challenges facing Russia any greater or more demanding of immediate answers. People might say to me, what about the war, or industrialization? Yes, those were also tough. But in those cases the issues on an intellectual level were simpler, it seems to me.

As far as I know, historians today are divided into conceptualists and positivists. The former use facts to build theories that they believe can predict the future. Thus, Marx came to the conclusion that capitalism in the monopolist stage destroys market economy and leads to a socialist planned economy. Lenin and Stalin decided that the management of such an economy must be modeled on a large factory and tried to realize this scheme in Russia. Their experience armed the positivists against similar theories and prompted them to conclude that theories must be abandoned completely: they would rely on facts, events, short connections between those, but not on guesses.

But the human desire to understand the road that leads to the future is inextinguishable. There will be new attempts, I'm sure, to build concepts arising from earlier institutions and the analysis of the possibilities of transforming them in changing circumstances. As an example, I will mention *Violence and*

Social Orders by North, Wallis, and Weingast, published in translation by the Gaidar Institute in 2011. Modern liberal democracy (or, in their terminology, the order of open access) is a complex of institutions that results from the desire of elites to reduce violence. Their ideas are supported by historical examples.

Similar ideas are expressed in this book by Gaidar and Chubais. But here the basis is historical material, as they examine the most important crossroads in Russian history between 1929 and 2009 and the circumstances of their passage—the choice of political decisions and the consequences, including institutions, that result. The result of the political decisions made in the late 1920s and early 1930s was the Soviet planned-administrative economy and the growing crisis that led to the crossroads of the 1990s. The decisions made in 1992–93 led to the creation of the market economy in Russia, a new stage in the country's development.

Let me give you an example from the book—the liberalization of prices. Critics maintain that it was done to suit a liberal scheme, the "Washington consensus," and that it caused great harm to the country. The actual situation in the country was that the supply of grain in the major cities would last only until February or March 1992, and the harvest in Russia begins in July. There was no hard currency for buying food abroad. Currency circulation had been disrupted over the previous years, and after the GKChP (State Committee on the State of Emergency, which tried to take control of the country away from Gorbachev) putsch a number of republics that had declared their independence printed money without permission of the central bank. But there was grain in the country. This crossroads presented two situations which required a choice:

1. Either take wheat away from kolkhozes by force and retain state prices, or liberalize prices, making it profitable to sell wheat to the state. (I should add that the government had little force and even less desire to use it, as the Bolsheviks had done in 1919.)

2. Address the disruption in currency circulation by introducing a national currency and putting off liberalization of prices to prevent high inflation, or liberalize prices as soon as possible and then take measures on financial stabilization.

There was no real choice. Prices were liberalized on 2 January 1992. There was a high price to pay in the form of inflation, which reached 2,600 percent. It was not until March that correspondent accounts could be set up for the central banks of union republics, treating their new currency emissions as technical credits. A national currency was introduced in August 1993. But here is the important part: the liberalization of prices in foreign trade together with the introduction of freedom of domestic trade in Russia removed the acuteness of the goods shortage, first of all. And second, we acquired a most important institution of market economy, free prices. Other necessary complementary institutions came a bit later.

Much later, in 2010, I had occasion to ask Leszek Balcerowicz, the author of the Polish market reforms, whether he had known about the Washington consensus in 1990. He said he had not.

I do not intend to retell the contents of the book in my preface. The episode I described is one of the most vivid and edifying in that brief time span in which were concentrated the most significant events and the authors' major acts. In that short time, around five hundred days, the institutional bases of a market economy were created in Russia. I can say this with assurance, because by mid-1993 the biggest part of the path to mass privatization, the great work of Anatoly Chubais, had been achieved. His other major work—financial stabilization—was accomplished in the next period, 1995–97, but it was less involved in the formation of institutions of a market economy. In sum, however, liberalization, privatization, and financial stabilization were the vital nucleus. That is the most important accomplishment of the two marvelous men who have written this book. Those who still consider them at fault for almost all the woes of our country must read it. As they do, they should consider that immediate impressions and lightweight judgments must make way for balanced reflection, in particular about the fact that the true significance of important political decisions is usually seen not instantly but over a long time and gradually. The flowering of the Russian market economy is yet to come—I believe that.

The more time that elapses between an event and the description of it, the less significant the event itself becomes and the greater the influence of the current political reality on how we perceive the event. The authors no longer took direct part in setting state policy after 1999. Their opinions are still extremely interesting, but there are more issues that I would like to discuss with them. The authors write about the crossroads encountered by the new leadership after Boris Yeltsin left: (1) whether to implement the economic reforms elaborated for Yeltsin's second term but not yet accomplished, or reject them; (2) after the end of the transformational crisis and transition to restored growth, whether to create instruments that could solve financial problems in unfavorable conditions, or use the resources coming from the rapid rise in oil prices to solve current problems. The third crossroads they describe is agreement or conflict between the state and big business, an issue with which Chubais had to deal starting in 1997, when he made his second appearance in the government. Here the problem is presented as "victory at Svyazinvest," while actually it was only one battle in a war that was just beginning.

In my view, these tightly interconnected crossroads objectively signaled the transition from the stage of market reforms and transformational crisis to the stage of liberalization of the Russian economy on market principles. Here the main question was what would be the main motive forces of modernization. Would it be high business activity, a maximal use of the opportunities of entrepreneurship awakened by the reforms? Or would it be the initiatives and resources of the state, that is, the bureaucracy, which thirsted for revenge against the oligarchs who thought so highly of themselves? The second option was the more usual, in line with the old Russian tradition, and it seemed less risky. By that point the authors had no influence over policy decisions, and the choice was made in favor of the second way. I am discussing this not because I think that Gaidar and Chubais did not understand the importance of this crossroads. They even write about it, albeit glancingly. It's just that I can say directly what they had difficulty saying out loud for political reasons. But it needs to be said, because we are still at this crossroads today. There's a reason we've started talking again about modernization and the investment climate. In the "fat years" these topics didn't seem timely.

Yet it is clear that the market economy was needed to replace the planned economy so that private initiative and high levels of business activity could be the basic forces for lifting up our economy. If we do not create beneficial opportunities for these forces, then oil revenues should be placed primarily into reserves, ready for good and bad situations; otherwise either we will generate inflation or we will not have the means to prevent yet another financial catastrophe. I hope that this comment of mine will add insight to the corresponding sections of the book.

In conclusion, I would like to draw your attention to the crossroads of our time. First, should conservative financial and monetary policies be preserved or not? The authors believe they definitely should be preserved. Investments and development are basically the work of private business, not of the state.

Second, innovation or degradation? I agree with them that an innovation economy and the creation of its preconditions is the natural choice, which requires only time and serious effort.

The authors warn that "logical constructs along the lines of 'Let's wait until they create a democratic political system for us and then we'll start creating an innovation economy' are totally unacceptable." Perhaps they had me in mind. It is true that I believe it is impossible to create a modern market economy without democracy. But I agree that we should not insist on preconditions but rather work in parallel, moving consecutively on both fronts. But eventually the time will come when further progress toward a market economy will be impossible without democratization. In essence, this is the conclusion with which Gaidar and Chubais end their book.

They are marvelous people and this is a marvelous book. I am un homme engagé and I love them. I do not consider them marvelous because I love them; just the reverse. In the early 1990s I did not know them well. But I understood what had to be done for our country. Therefore I could appreciate their accomplishments. I hope that with time, more and more of my fellow citizens will come to understand and appreciate them, too.

From the Author

Anatoly Chubais

It's an extremely acute sensation, understanding that an enormous country is at a historic crossroads and must choose a path within days or even hours. It's the stuff of Russian fairy tales: "Go you left, and … Go you right, and …" The difference is that we are talking not about a legendary hero but about almost 150 million people, many of whom have no idea that their fate and perhaps their lives are being decided at that moment. In the 1990s our country faced this situation at least four times. It just so happened that in some of those moments we—Yegor Gaidar, I, and our whole team—had a direct connection to the decision.

Perhaps that is how this book came about, particularly since we had not planned to write it. We had to analyze many times, especially in recent years, what we had done right and what was wrong. But in making the analysis, we had to understand not only what was done but what was avoided. This is particularly important in watershed eras when the political corridor is very narrow and almost always the choice involves picking the least bad scenario out of a variety of bad ones.

Yegor Gaidar was not only an outstanding economist but also a profound historian. He died just after completing his part of the book, at the age of fifty-four. Now, in 2011, I am amazed to see how much of what he wrote about in early 2009 is taking place before our very eyes in the economic and political dynamics of our country, Europe, and the United States. This is one more example of the fact that history teaches. It teaches at least those who are not indifferent to it.

And it is for them that we wrote this book.

Introduction

The concept of historical determinism, according to which developed countries show the less-developed ones a picture of their future, is a key element in Marxist theory, which had a serious influence on social thought of the nineteenth and twentieth centuries. The concept holds that history has its laws and is predetermined. The question is only when the inevitable will happen.

For decades in our country this concept was part of the ideology of the powers that be. In fact, systemic changes that occur in the societies of more developed countries—involving per capita gross domestic product, urbanization, structure of employment, level of education, birth rate, longevity, and political systems—look like those that take place decades later in less developed ones. So there is undoubtedly a grain of truth in Karl Marx's classic works. But twentieth-century experiences have shown the limits of historical determinism.

Though there are general patterns, the development of countries is not strictly predetermined. What happens in countries catching up does not always repeat the experience of the countries leading world economic growth. This can be seen in the fact that the first large-scale socialist experiment was attempted not in England, the most developed country of the nineteenth century, but in Russia, which could hardly be considered a leader of economic development in the early twentieth century.

In history, the past turns to stone. Historians always want to show that the events fit the pattern. During the Soviet regime numerous works were published dedicated to the inevitability of revolution in Russia. But almost no one wrote about it before the enormous tsarist regime collapsed. The early 1990s saw many books about the inevitability of the collapse of the socialist regime in the USSR. But almost none of the authors had ever mentioned the possibility of such an event before the mid-1980s.

It is trite to mention that history has no subjunctive mood, but it is true. What happened, happened. However, as people who were part of the decision-making process around key issues in Russian policy, we can attest that imagining that everything that has happened was inevitable would be inaccurate. Without understanding this, it is difficult to evaluate the events in our country and in the world during the last few decades.

It would be incorrect to discuss the crossroads of the late and post-Soviet periods without recalling the alternatives that faced the leadership of the Soviet state from the late 1920s to the mid-1960s. We will begin with the main crossroads in Russian history after the revolution of 1917–22.

1928–1984

The key decision in the postrevolutionary period was the policy on the peasantry, made in 1928–29. By 1926 the New Economic Policy, the essence of which was the combination of the authoritarian rule of the Communist Party and the dominance of state property in industry with relatively free trade and a stable currency supported by gold, had fully justified itself. After a period of turbulent restorative growth in 1923–24, Russia continued developing, albeit not as dynamically (Fig. 1).

The greatest obstacle to further acceleration of economic growth was politics. The Communist regime, which had taken power in an agrarian country and whose ideology was based in great part on the French Revolution, feared a repeat of the Vendée and the development of events along the lines of the French scenario after the collapse of the Jacobin dictatorship in 1794. Hence the wary attitude toward the well-to-do peasantry, in those days called kulaks, who had invested in their homesteads. This led to the repressive policies that stripped them of voting rights. Bear in mind that in the 1920s rural residents made up

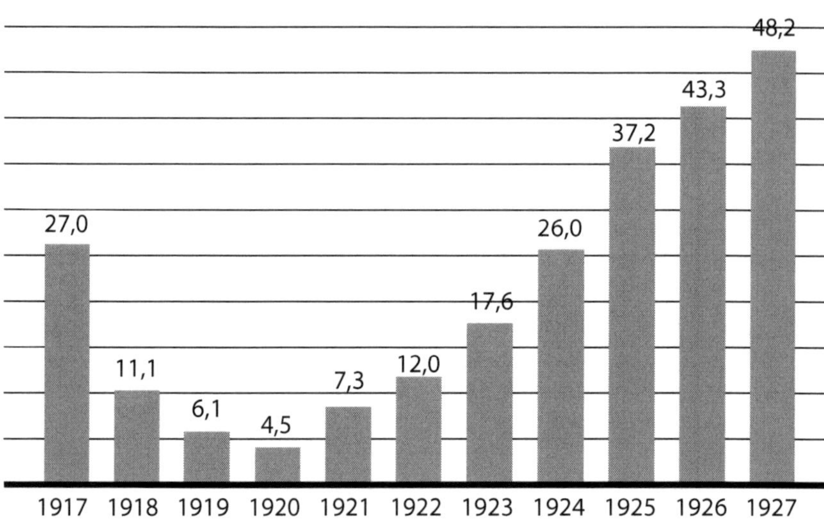

Figure 1. Gross industrial production in Russia (volume in 2000 prices, in billions of rubles)
Source: V. M. Simchera, Razvitie ekonomiki Rossii za 100 let. Istoricheskie riady, vekovye trendy, institutsional'nye tsikly (Moscow: Nauka, 2006), 325

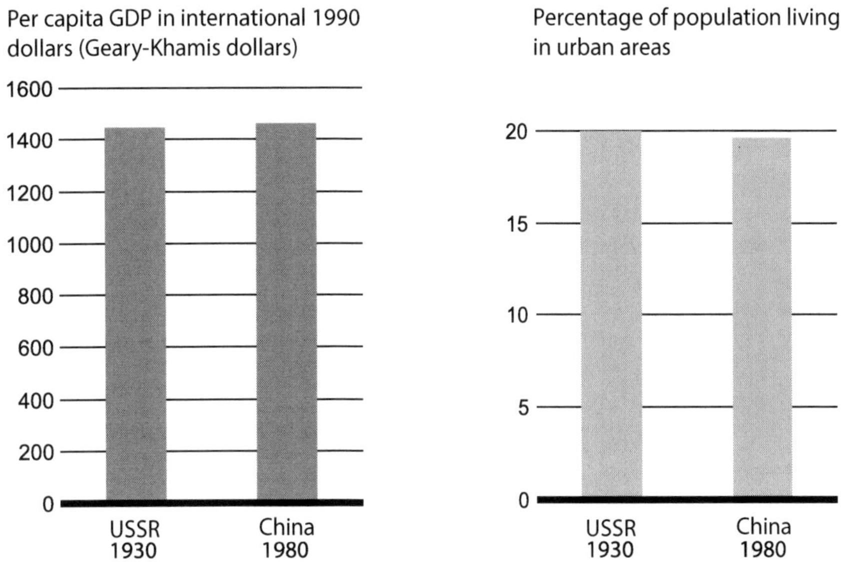

Figure 2. Comparison of the USSR in 1930 and China in 1980 (per capita GDP and percentage of population living in urban areas)

the majority of Russia's population: in 1926 the figure was 82.1 percent, and in 1928–29 it was 80.1 percent.[1]

When you explain to a person who is hardworking and not stupid that if he develops his homestead he will encounter difficulties, his reaction is not hard to predict. He will limit himself to a decently organized farm oriented toward personal consumption and will not get involved in investment escapades. Yet the country needed forced industrialization. The world was moving forward. The fate of the country and its ruling regime depended on the speed with which industrialization took place in the Soviet Union.

The essence of this historic crossroads: repeal the discriminatory measures toward the most advanced part of the peasantry, or collectivize it by force?

The first path meant a change in policy toward those who were prepared to develop production and employ modern technology, that is, the kulaks. It presumed the preservation of money stability, markets, institutions, and ensuring the authoritarian regime of the Communist Party. Decades later this path came to be called the "Chinese way." The decision on whether to take this path was made in the Soviet Union at an economic level very close to the one that characterized China at the start of Deng Xiaoping's reforms (Fig. 2).

1 Narodnoe khoziaistvo SSSR v 1956 godu. Stat. ezhegodnik (Moscow: State Statistical Publishing House, 1957).

The frankest formulation of this scenario of development came from Nikolai Bukharin, chief ideologist of the party, in his 1925 article "Enrich Yourselves!" Subsequently, for political reasons, Bukharin was forced to renounce his own words. But in the course of debate in 1928–29, his position, like that of Alexei Rykov, head of the Soviet government, did not change.

The second path was proposed by Joseph Stalin. Essentially his solution for accelerating economic growth was to expropriate grain from the countryside at prices lower than what the peasants wanted to charge; this amounted to forced collectivization, that is, the reestablishment of serfdom in a new guise. In this version of development, the peasant became a second-class citizen whose income was many times lower than that of city dwellers and who was deprived of such social guarantees as a pension. Thus the peasants were given a powerful stimulus to change their status by immigrating to the cities. They could do it by joining the army or working on shock construction projects.

For Bukharin, the most important argument for choosing the strategy of economic and political development was that in a country where the basis of the army is the peasantry, it was impossible to compel the army to forcibly take away grain in the countryside.[2] But Stalin proved it was possible. The cost of the choice at this historic crossroads was high—millions of kulaks exiled to Siberia, millions of peasant starved to death in 1932–33.

Yet another crossroads of the socialist period involved choosing the path of development of agriculture after Stalin's death.

This problem faced the Soviet government in 1953–57. By 1953 the agricultural crisis, related to the policy selected in 1928–29 to enslave the peasantry, was reality.[3] But there are no documents to confirm the intention of some of the leaders of the party and state to follow the path chosen in 1979 by Deng Xiaoping, that is, to break up the kolkhozes.

Nikita Khrushchev proposed returning to an idea that had been popular in the early 1930s: developing virgin soils and reclaiming fallow land. His oppo-

---

2 See Kak lomali NEP: Stenogrammy plenumov TsK VKP(b) 1928–1929 gg., ed. A. N. Yakovlev (Moscow: MFD, 2000), vol. 4.

3 This is how Nikita Khrushchev characterized the situation: "Let me cite a few figures. In 1940, the state had purchased 2,225 million poods of grain, and only 1,850 poods in 1953—that is, 375 million poods less. At the same time, in connection with the general growth of agriculture, the significant increase in the urban population, the growth of real income the use of bread products grew annually. … The demand for export increased both for consumer grains and for fodder; however, the lack of grain caused the export for 1954 to be set at 190 million poods (3,120,000 tons) while the demand was for 293 million poods (4,800,000 tons)." See Report by N. S. Khrushchev to the Presidium of the CC CPSU, 22 January 1954; N. S. Khrushchev, Stroitel'stvo kommunizma v SSSR i razvitie sel'skogo khoziaistva. Rechi i dokumenty, v 5 t. [Building communism in the USSR and the development of agriculture. Speeches and documents in 5 volumes], 1:85, 8.

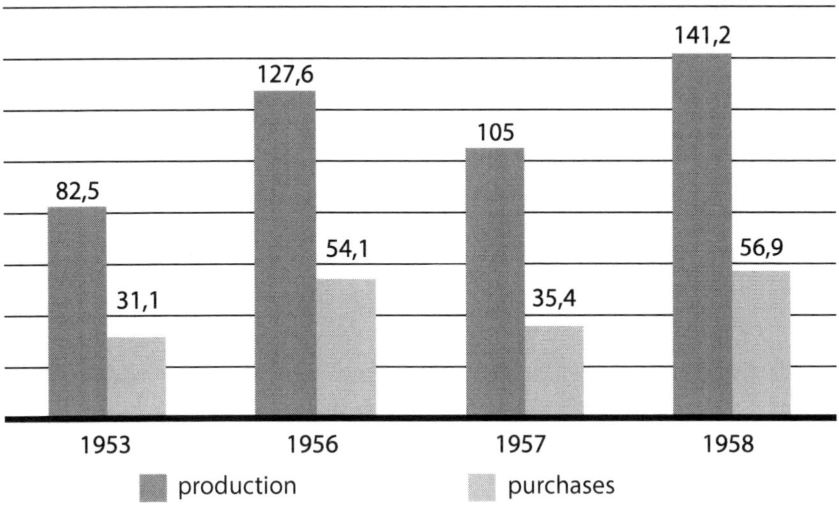

Figure 3. Average annual production and purchase of grain in the USSR in 1953–58 (millions of tons)

Source: Narodnoe khoziaistvo SSR v 1959 godu. Stat. ezhegodnik (Moscow: Gosstatizdat TsSU SSSR, 1960), 314–15, 322–23

nents proposed investing in increasing the productivity of agriculture in central Russia.[4] Khrushchev's point of view won out. In the short run its implementation yielded results that were not too bad (Fig. 3).

However, in the long term, it was dangerous: the dependence of the grain supply on weather increased in regions that previously had been virgin or long fallow. At the same time, the crisis in agriculture in central Russia continued to grow worse.

Another crossroads that arose in 1953–57: to what degree should the political regime be liberalized and move away from mass repressions?

The arrest and execution of Lavrenti Beria and the tone of discussion at the Plenum of the Central Committee of the Communist Party of the Soviet Union (CPSU) on 22–29 June 1957 showed that that the struggle over this question

4 Unexpectedly for Khrushchev, expert scientists spoke out at the 1954 Plenum against the virgin soils program. Their recommendations called for introducing the use of steam [for pest control] and crop rotation, sowing perennial grasses, combining grain production with animal husbandry, and using shallow plowing from the very start; they stressed the importance of pure steam. Khrushchev rejected outright the recommendations of these experts (Professor M. G. Chizhevskaya, T. S. Mal'tsev, and others) and supported the incompetent advice of T. Lysenko (who was president of VASKHNIL). See I. E. Zelnin, "Agrarnaia politika N. S. Khrushcheva i sel'skoe khoziastvo strany" [N. S. Khrushchev's agrarian policy and the country's agriculture], Otechestvennaia istoriia 1 (2000): 79.

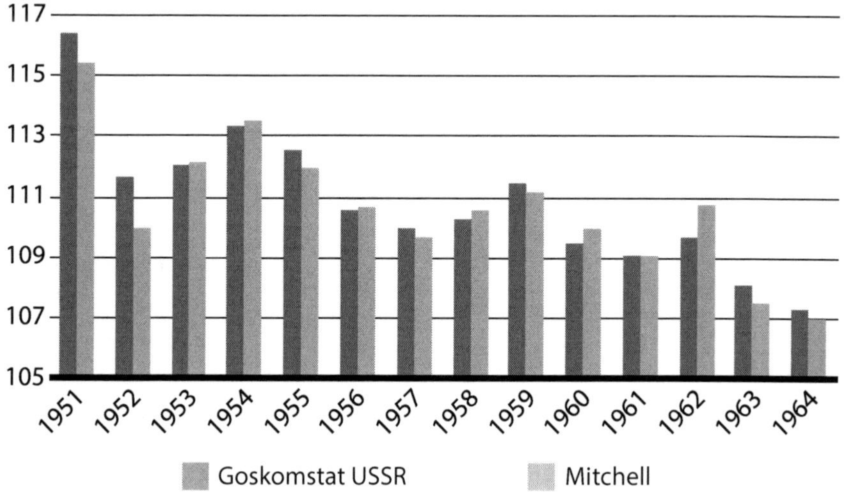

Figure 4. Rates of growth in industrial production in Russia, 1951–64 (percentage of the previous year)

Sources: Narodnoe khoziaistvo SSSR. Stat. sboronik (Moscow: Statistika, various years); B. R. Mitchell, International Historical Statistics: Europe 1750–1993, 4th ed. (London: Palgrave Macmillan, 2000), 424; R. Moorsteen and R. P. Powell, The Soviet Capital Stock, 1928–1962 (Homewood, IL: Richard D. Irwin, 1996)

was fierce. The essence of the alternatives is simple: maintain the repressive regime, which might take as its next victims people who were part of the regime, or liberalize it to some degree, in order to guarantee life and liberty at least for the country's leadership. The majority of the ruling elite supported Khrushchev in choosing the second way. This was manifested vividly at the 1957 Plenum, when the military, headed by Marshal Zhukov, did not allow Khrushchev to be removed from power.

The liberalization of the regime had serious economic consequences. The economy, not market but state, could produce results only in conditions of total fear of repressions. But it was impossible to guarantee the life and freedom of the leaders without loosening the repressions against ordinary citizens. And when the fear was gone, new problems arose in the economy.[5]

By 1965 it was clear that there were problems in Soviet agriculture. Symptomatic was the transition from being a large net exporter of grain, which Russia had been for many decades, to being a net importer. The rates of industrial

---

5 Khrushchev, after a visit to the Donbass mining region, described the situation at the Presidium of the Central Committee of the CPSU on 24 August 1956 with the succinct phrase "They're swiping everything." See RGANI, f. 3, op. 12, D. 1005, L. 21–23; quoted from Prezidium TsK KPSS: 1954–1964: Chernovye protokol'nye zapisi zasedanii. Stenogrammy. Postanovleniia, 2nd ed., 1:160.

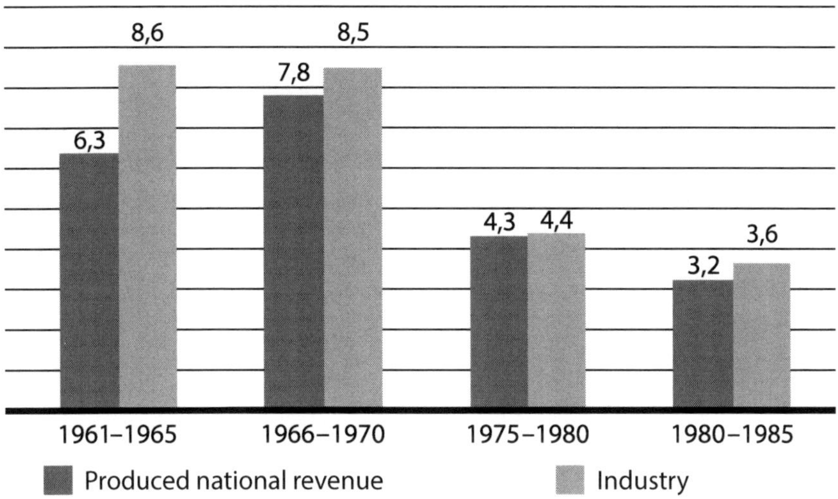

Figure 5. Average annual rate of increase in national revenue and industrial production in the USSR, 1961–85 (percent)

Source: Narodnoe khoziaistvo SSSR. Stat. sbornik (Moscow: Statistika, various years)

growth slowed as well, as measured both by Soviet and expert Western statistics (Fig. 4).

It was obvious that something had to be done with the system of managing the Soviet economy. Hence the arrival at a new historic crossroads, which boiled down to the selection of strategy and arsenal of reforms.

The essence of the reforms proposed by Alexei Kosygin, chairman of the government, was a group of cautious measures to increase the role of market mechanisms in the economy. For all their limited nature, the reforms created impressive results. The five-year phase 1966–70 was one of the most successful in the late Soviet period (Fig. 5).

Even limited measures to encourage enterprises to link profit with investment and to provide workers with incentives for successful outcomes yielded results.

This crossroads was overlaid by another one: what was to be done with Eastern Europe?

This region, which came under Soviet dominion as a result of World War II, was closely integrated into European civilization. It was better developed economically than the USSR. However, after the events in East Germany in 1953 and in Hungary in 1956, it had been clear that the USSR was prepared to use force to maintain its control over Eastern Europe. Now, signs of liberalization in the Soviet regime gave people hope that liberalization of the political regime and even market reforms were possible in their own countries.

In Hungary the liberalization of the regime came after the events of 1956, and by 1967 they were discussing a program of limited market reforms. Therefore it was quite natural for neighboring Czechoslovakia's new government to try to combine market reforms with political liberalization. However, the Soviet government realized that this might bring NATO control of Czechoslovakia and violation of the cooperation with Soviet troops in Hungary, Poland, and East Germany. It could not allow that. Besides, the presence in a socialist country of a regime that chose an alternative path of development combining democracy and market economy was unacceptable to the Soviet leadership. The result was the decision to invade Czechoslovakia.

Foreign and domestic policy are interrelated. Invading Czechoslovakia affected affairs inside the USSR. The party leaders became more entrenched in their conviction that experimenting with liberalizing the regime and market reforms was dangerous and could lead to the loss of power. The economic reforms begun in the mid-1960s were stopped. At the same time, the discovery of major oil deposits in western Siberia helped compensate for the losses created by inefficient agriculture and the forced mass imports of food.

1985–1991

By the early 1980s, the Soviet economy had stagnated (Fig. 6). The country had become one of the largest importers of agricultural produce (Fig. 7).

It was obvious that the economy had lost its dynamism. The Politburo of the CPSU's Central Committee formed the Commission on Improving the Management of the Economy, headed by chairman of the government N. Tikhonov. Its task was to elaborate measures that could restore the rate of economic development. The political regime was not very popular, but it was established. There was the chance that the measures it proposed and imposed on the society would be accepted without serious resistance.

D. Gvishiani was appointed head of the Scientific Section; he was the son-in-law of former prime minister Alexei Kosygin and deputy chairman of the Committee of Science and Technology. The directors of the major economic institutions of the USSR were members of the section. Gvishiani proposed to the country's leadership a program of cautious economic reforms.

By that time, it was too late to take the Chinese path of development. The employment structure and the portion of the rural population were different. They explored a different alternative—implementing economic reforms similar to those done in Yugoslavia and Hungary. The leaders of the economic bloc of the CPSU Secretariat examined the proposal and informed Gvishiani that this economic policy went beyond the borders of political reality: in fact, it was talking about instituting market socialism (even though the term was not used in the text), and that was unacceptable because of ideological considerations.[6] Note that this conversation took place before the sharp drop in the prices for oil and gas, our country's most important exports—that is, before the acute and profound economic crisis in the USSR.

By the mid-1980s, the USSR had become one of the largest importers of grain. Because of the low efficiency of kolkhoz agriculture, cities could be supplied only through imports. The USSR paid for imported grain by exporting oil, petroleum products, gas, and metals. The amount of manufactured goods available for export was very limited because of their low quality. But in the

6 Commentary to the final version of "General Concept of Development of the Economic Mechanism of Enterprises and Associations," 30 July 1985, from E. I. Kapustin, director of the Institute of the Economy of the Academy of Sciences USSR, to Academician D. M. Gvishiani, deputy chairman of Gosplan USSR.

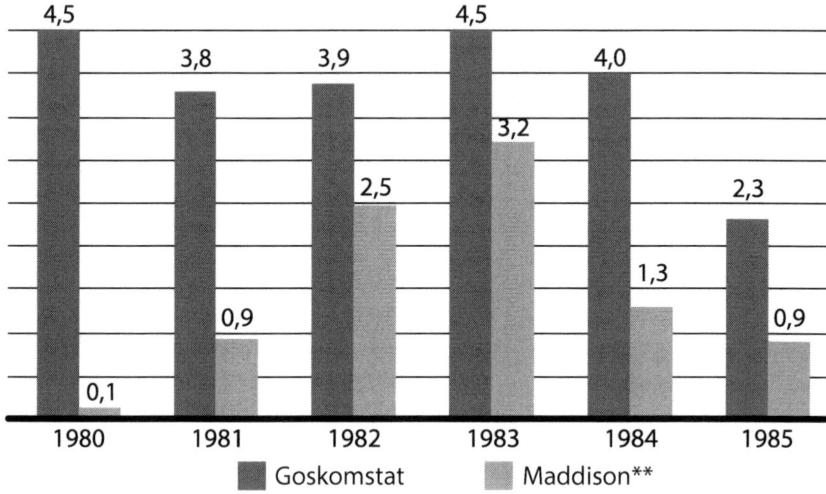

Figure 6. Growth rate of USSR gross national product,* 1980–85 (percentage of previous year)

* Rate of increase of GNP, USSR

* Based on volume of GNP USSR in international 1990 dollars (Geary-Khamis dollars)

Note: According to Gur Ofer's data, the average annual GNP growth in the USSR between 1980 and 1985 was 2 percent.

Sources: Narodnoe khoziaistvo SSSR v 1988. Stat. sbornik (Moscow: Finansy i statistika, 1989); Maddison's Historical Statistics (long historical views), www.ggdc.net/madison; G. Ofer, "Soviet Economic Growth, 1928–1985," Journal of Economic Literature 25, no. 4 (1987): 1767–833

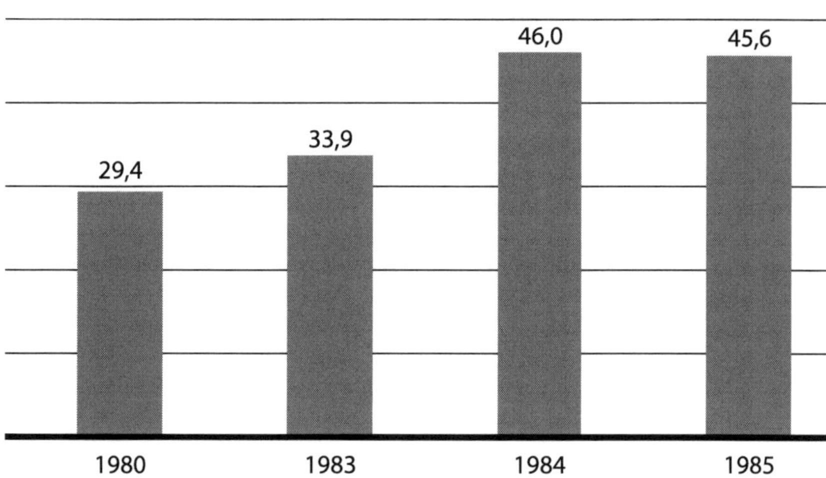

Figure 7: Import of grain by the USSR, 1980–85* (millions of tons)

* Data for grain imports 1981–82 are missing.

Source: Sotsialisticheskie strany i strany kapitalizma v 1986 godu. Stat. sbornik (Moscow: Statistika, 1987)

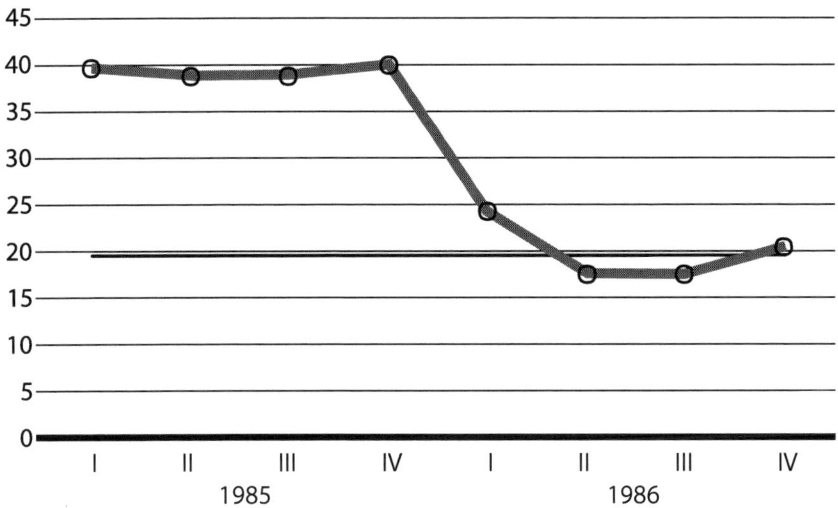

Figure 8. Quarterly dynamics of oil prices in 1985–86 against the average historical level (in 2000 prices, dollars per barrel)
Source: IMF, International Financial Statistics, 2004

period between August 1985 and May 1986, oil prices dropped by half (Fig. 8) and revenue from oil exports fell sharply.

The Soviet leadership was at a crossroads: how to react to the sharply changed foreign economic and financial situation?

The first option was to raise prices sharply on food. However, this would mean the violation of an unspoken and unwritten understanding between the authorities and the populace. Its essence, formed after the rejection of mass repressions, was that the people will not ask why you are in power even though we never elected you, and the authorities will guarantee stability in the people's life, with one of the elements being stability in prices of the most important consumer goods.

The second option was to reduce spending on arms production and on maintaining the army and investments. This path meant inevitable conflict with the power structures and the economic elite as well as the growth of social problems in one-industry cities.

The third option was to stop supplying Eastern Europe with oil under barter contracts and instead send it to countries capable of paying for it with hard currency. But that meant disbanding the East European part of the Soviet empire and a rejection of the results of World War II.

The fourth option was to do nothing besides borrow money from the West, preserve the existing import structure, and hope that prices for raw materials

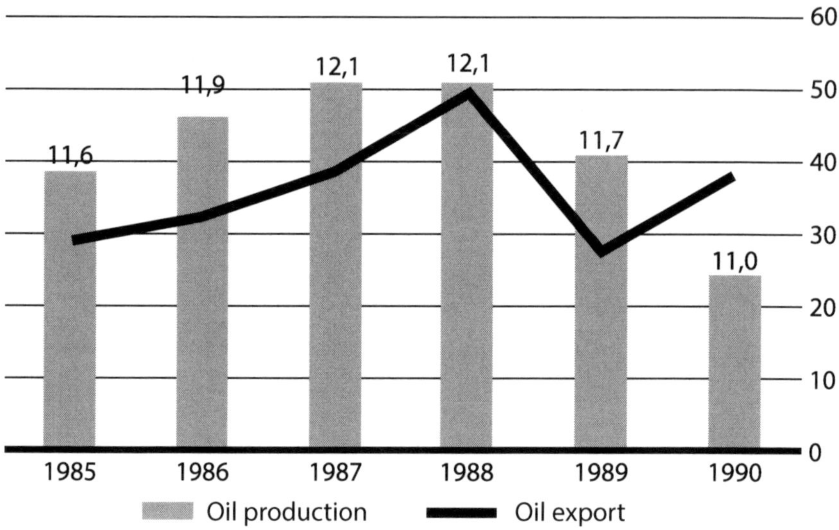

Figure 9. Oil production in the USSR (millions of barrels a day, bars) and export of oil from the USSR for freely convertible currency (millions of tons, right side), 1985–90

Sources: U.S. Department of Energy; Narodnoe khoziaistvo SSSR v 1990. Stat. sbornik (Moscow: Finansy i statistika, 1991), 646

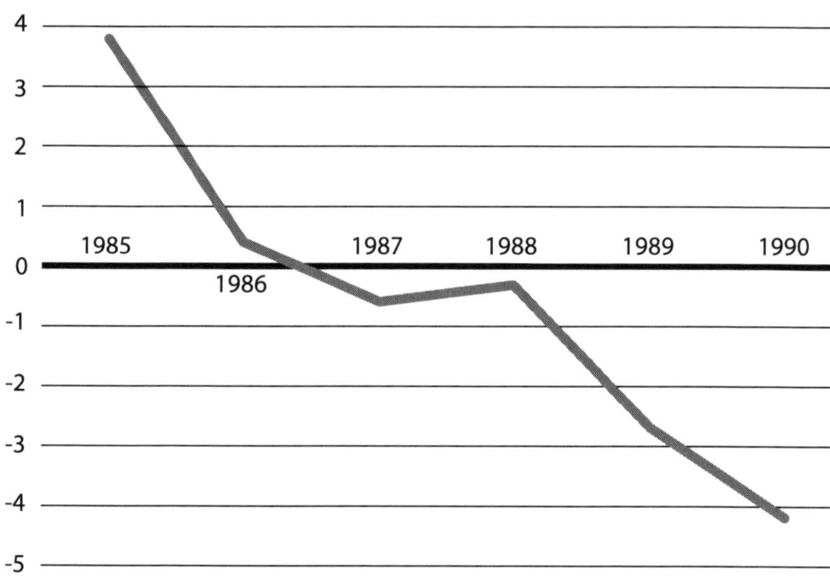

Figure 10. Growth increase in industrial production in the USSR, 1985–90 (percentage of previous year)

Source: Narodnoe khoziaistvo SSSR. Stat. ezhegodnik (Moscow: Finansy i statistika, 1995, 1988, 1990)

would go up again. That's the one that was chosen, and we know the result (Figs. 9 and 10).

By 1988–89 it was clear that there were fewer opportunities to attract commercial credits from Western financial markets. Then such opportunities stopped coming at all. This made an acute crisis in the Soviet economy inevitable.

This led to yet another crossroads at the end of the 1980s: political liberalization or harshening of the regime?

If it was impossible to maintain the conditions of the unspoken agreement that had been in place for decades, then the political regime could be softened in the hopes of coming to terms with society. Or, on the contrary, they could increase the repressions, which would mean heightened conflict with the West and a complete loss of any chance to get state credits from the West. This policy might also provoke the development of events on the model of early 1917 in Russia. However, political liberalization in the presence of an economic crisis created serious risks for the stability of the regime.

They chose liberalization. Probably what Georgy Plekhanov had called "the role of the personality in history" had played its part.[7] Mikhail Gorbachev did not want bloodshed and repressions.

The deepening economic crisis against the background of liberalization of the regime and the first relatively free, albeit manipulated, elections in 1989 demanded the implementation of profound economic reforms that would change the very essence of the existing system of managing the economy.

* * *

By the late 1980s three ideological platforms were being presented in a more or less structured form. The first demanded the reinstatement of order "like Stalin," though harsh repressions. The second boiled down to the thesis "Lenin was good, Stalin was bad." Lenin's "war communism" of 1918–20 was viewed as being forced, while the turn to the New Economic Policy was deemed the "true Leninist" course. This platform supported "socialism with a human face," market socialism. The third platform was capitalism, the path of development based on private property, the market, and democracy.

These platforms defined not only the political crossroads but the economic one: how do you reform the economic system of socialism once it has fallen into crisis?

Each platform had its history. Seventy years of total brainwashing and the Iron Curtain that shut off the country from the world stood behind the Stalinist

7 G. V. Plekhanov, K voprosu o roli lichnosti v istorii [Concerning the role of personality in history], vol. 2 of Izbrannye filosofskie proizvedeniia [Selected philosophical works] (Moscow, 1956).

ideology. The Stalinists were not only in the CPSU's Central Committee, the KGB, and the military-industrial complex. By the mid-1980s you could see a picture of Stalin in many car windshields. The Stalinists had a strong position in the political scene, as shown by the GKChP putsch in 1991. But this economic logic would have contradicted the political vector chosen by Gorbachev, oriented toward glasnost and perestroika. The attempt to turn back the economy as politics moved forward would have been too contradictory for that period.

After the 1968 events in Czechoslovakia, the ideology of market socialism had gone underground. But the best intellectuals of Soviet economic thought (Abel Aganbegyan, Tatiana Zaslavskaya, Stanislav Shatalin, Gavriil Popov, Nikolai Petrakov, Pavel Bunich, and many others) continued to defend the idea of market socialism. By the mid-1980s this ideological platform had benefited from twenty-five years of development, the sympathy of the majority of the intelligentsia, and the authority of part of the party and government circles.

Ideas were developed within its framework that were partially realized in the course of the Kosygin reforms in the mid-1960s and which were found in the proposals of the Gvishiani Commission, rejected by the party leaders in 1985. They were directed at strengthening the economic independence of state enterprises, the expansion of the rights of labor collectives, and a cautious change in property rights—the introduction of rent and permission to form cooperatives.

These ideas began to be implemented. In 1987–88 the paradigm of market socialism was manifested in the laws on state enterprises (associations), on "cooperation", and on rent. All these were half measures: the expansion of the rights of state enterprises did not revoke planned assignments and did not offer the enterprises real freedom in pricing, and the official pluralism of forms of property did not give a true start to the formation of the institution of private property in the country. The very term "market socialism" was in fact banned until the late 1980s.

The halfhearted nature of these reforms was also dangerous because it was not supported by measures for financial stabilization. On the contrary, the unlimited supply of money in combination with the preservation of regulated prices for products of state enterprises and the out-of-control cooperative sector led to colossal disproportions that destroyed the country's economy.

The continuing contradictions and difficulties in realizing the concept of "market socialism" in the USSR were supplemented by no less acute strategic issues, including how to guarantee an appropriate level and efficiency of investments. Yugoslavia faced that problem, as its market economy was based essentially on cooperative property. Analogous problems arose in production cooperatives all over the world. Everywhere the owners, who were also at the same time the enterprises' workers, voted to increase prices and raise wages rather than lower the cost of production and use income or profit for investment. They preferred to consume today rather than invest in new technology that would pay for itself only in just a few years, an approach that made modernization of the

Table 1

Question: "Do you support or not support the following measures by the Russian leadership?"

Measure	Support	Do not support	No answer
Accelerated privatization of housing	64%	17%	19%
Accelerated privatization of state enterprises	44%	34%	22%
Permission to buy and sell land freely	54%	30%	16%
Move to free-market prices	26%	56%	18%

Source: S. P. Shpil'ko, L. A. Khakhulina, Z. V. Kupriyanova, V. V. Bodrova, L. G. Zubova, N. P. Kovaleva, M. D. Krasil'nikova, and T. V. Avdeenko, Otsenka naseleniem sotsial-no-ekonomicheskoj situatsii v strane (po rezul-tatam sotsiologicheskikh oprosov 1991 goda). Nauchnyj doklad (Moscow: VTsIOM, 1991), 8

enterprises much more difficult. In the framework of socialism, even market socialism, this contradiction was unresolvable.

The half measures and contradictory nature of market socialism became increasingly apparent by the end of the 1980s. And even though in official economics and in the press there remained a taboo on open discussion of these problems, dozens of programs to overcome the limitations of market socialism were discussed first privately and then more or less openly. The details of the steps and the order in which they were taken varied, but the substance was the same: legalization of private property, privatization of state property, liberalization of prices, restoration of market mechanisms, integration of the country into the world economy, introduction of the convertible ruble, financial stabilization, and the demonopolization of the economy.

The political moment was unique because in 1991 the majority of Russians, according to VTsIOM polls, saw that the economy was falling apart and were prepared to support all these measures except the liberalization of prices (Table 1). However, without it any program of market reforms was doomed to failure. The leaders of the USSR understood this, but out of fear of a social explosion did not undertake price liberalization.

From here came a series of incomplete programs of economic reforms. The critical point came in the summer and early fall of 1990, with the discussions around the 500-Day Plan. Given the harsh economic crisis, the plan was too political and populist.[8] However, it also outlined the main actions necessary

8 "The main distinguishing feature is that it is based on a fundamentally new economic doctrine. The movement toward the market is primarily at the expense of the state, not ordinary people … The program's goal is: take everything possible from the state and give it to the people. There are serious reasons to suppose that returning a significant part of property and resources to the people on varying conditions will guarantee their much more effective use and will help avoid many negative phenomena in the process of transitioning to

to stabilize the economy and change the economic system—privatization, financial stabilization, liberalization of prices, demonopolization, and integration into the global economy. The program created a base of political cooperation between the head of state, Soviet president Mikhail Gorbachev, and Boris Yeltsin, chairman of the Supreme Soviet of the Russian Soviet Federative Socialist Republic (RSFSR), a charismatic politician who was more popular than Gorbachev, at least in Russia.

In our opinion, this was the last chance to implement regulated reforms that might have saved the Soviet Union. But most of the party economic elite was against the 500-Day Plan. The plan had no chance of being realized because it included such points as sharply reducing expenditures on the military complex.[9]

---

the market. It is necessary to decisively reduce all state expenditures, including on budget lines hidden from society … Another fundamental feature of the program is that people do not have to wait for someone's permission and instructions but act in accordance with their own interests. The program shows the best way to act in that direction. A person reading this program with interest can determine what is good for him personally and decide ahead of time what should be done as well as when, what, and how much he must demand, and under what terms and from whom, in order to realize his economic rights and interests. … Thus the program can be seen as a program for realizing the rights of citizens to a better, more dignified life. … The main goals of the reform are economic freedom for citizens and the creation on that basis of an efficient economic system, capable of guaranteeing the dynamic development of the economy and a worthy level of prosperity for the country's citizens, getting past the gap between other countries. … The most important task of state government on all levels and primarily on the republican and local levels is guaranteeing a high level of social security for citizens, understood on one hand as offering all citizens various possibilities to earn their own prosperous life and on the other hand as state support for members of society who cannot work or are at risk. … The financing of the Ministry of Defense USSR and the KGB is significantly reduced (up to 20%); in particular through severe cuts in purchases of arms and military construction while maintaining for a year the average wages for workers in the manufacturing plants. The saved material resources will be made available for free sale. No less than 30% of the economy of reduced spending for these items will be used to raise officers' salaries and the construction of housing for the military, including those moved to the USSR from other countries and moved to the reserves." "Programma '500 dnei,'" www.yabloko.ru/Publ/500/500-4.html.

9 "The basis for our calculations is the budget for the 4th quarter 1990, proposed by the Ministry of Finance USSR: income, 46.9 billion rubles, expenses, 62.5 billion rubles, deficit, 15.6 billion rubles.

"1. Reducing expenses:

"a) specific reductions: capital investments—20%; operating costs—30–50%; military expenses (for purchases of military technology)—50–70%; expenses on foreign economic activity (aid and loans to other countries should be frozen for a quarter at the 0 ruble level);

"b) creating 'protected' lines: socio-cultural events; support of law enforcement agencies; expenses for servicing state debt; expenses on elections for people's deputies of the USSR;

"c) reductions of all unprotected lines by 10–15%.

"The result: reduction of expenses on the union budget by 10 billion rubles." Transition to the Market: The 500 Day Plan (Moscow, 1990), 221.

The consequence was the strange military exercises outside Moscow in the fall of 1990.[10]

It was right after them that Gorbachev refused to support a program of economic reforms. That determined the further development of events.[11] They unfolded kaleidoscopically, and economic reform receded into the background, despite the unfolding destruction of the economic mechanism. Right up until August 1991, reform was replaced by complex political maneuvers and sometimes just the to-and-fro of Soviet leaders in the face of the growing threat of a military coup.

Having rejected the course of manageable market reforms, Gorbachev had to choose harshening political repressions. That was demonstrated in the Baltics in January 1991. Soviet newspapers described the events in Lithuania this way: "On 7 January paratrooper units were sent to Lithuania. On 8 January they began action. According to the commentator on the television program Vremya,

10 "At the Supreme Soviet USSR, People's Deputy S. Belozertsev raised a question regarding the 'strange' movements of military units around Moscow. On 9–10 September the Ryazan paratrooper regiment and parts of the Tula Division, the Drzerzhinsky MVD Division, were hastily made battle ready and then deployed; parts of the Pskov air paratrooper division were moved. The officers at first thought this was ordinary preparations, perhaps for parade or training. But the troops were given weapons, even though weapons are rarely distributed before exercises; even in training on the use of weapons, the armament is delivered at the last stage. The soldiers were worried. The students did not believe that the moved division with bulletproof vests and helmets was sent to harvest potatoes. The Russian government was not informed. None of the deputies who visited the units was allowed to meet with personnel. This is how events developed on the eve of the rally announced for 16 September in Moscow. According to People's Deputy RSFSR V. Ryumin, a unit of paratroopers from the Moscow region were present at the rally dressed in 'civvies.'

"Defense Minister D. Yazov, speaking at a session of the Supreme Soviet USSR, called all these facts falsification; however, he did confirm that the paratroopers did come to Moscow. The marshal first explained that the Ryazan and Kostroma regiments had come for the parade on Red Square, and then, without naming any other units, announced that there 'exercises had taken place.'" A. A. Pankratov, "Someone Thought There Were Exercises," Komsomolskaya Pravda, 26 September 1990; A. A. Pankratov, "The Marshal Responded There Are Exercises. But There Is Still No Clarity on the Paratroopers' March,"Komsomolskaya Pravda, 4 October 1990.

11 In January 1990 one of the authors of the 500-Day Plan described the potential scenario: "Our country will not be an exception. The general contours of the anti-inflation program are not hard to predict. The state's expenditures will go down on subsidies and first of all on food. Grain import will fall sharply. State investments, capitalization of enterprises, and production of investment products were stabilize on a low level. It is more complicated with defense spending: here it all depends on who will realize which program. Whether we manage to stabilize the economy, saving the sprouts of democratic and market institutions, a foreign policy open to the world, and the course for integration into the world economy, or see a spree of irresponsibility, demagoguery, and anarchy preparing the road once again to the dead end of a totalitarian regime and autarchy—the battle around this dilemma will be the main content of economic policy in the near future." Kommunist 1991, no. 2.

they 'took under guard' the House of Print and several other sites in the city. The House of Print was taken under guard with the use of firepower. There are wounded. Communications with Lithuania are stopped. The airport is closed, the trains are not running … On 11 January the chairman of Gosteleradio, Leonid Kravchenko, gave orders to stop broadcasting the news channels of the major independent news agency Interfax, whose services were used by many Western journalists in Moscow."[12]

V. Mikhailov, head of the Department of National Policy of the CPSU's Central Committee, briefed the leadership of the Central Committee on 11 January 1991 on the events in Lithuania: "According to reports from responsible workers of the C[entral] C[ommittee] CPSU (Comrades Kazyulin, Udovichenko), located in Lithuania, on 11 January of this year, the House of Print and DOSSAF [the site of the regional defense department]in Vilnius were taken under control of the paratroopers and in Kaunas the building of officers' training. This operation took place without major confrontations on the whole."[13]

These actions by the USSR's enforcement structures were met with energetic resistance. The parliaments of Russia, Ukraine, Belorussia, and Kazakhstan, as well as Mossovet and Lensovet, condemned the events. The miners' strike committees in Kuzbass demanded that the president of the USSR step down and that the Congress of People's Deputies be dissolved. The West, despite the crisis in Kuwait, made harsh statements addressed to the Soviet leadership. Gorbachev best expressed the situation at a session of the union parliament: "The situation smells of kerosene."[14]

Yuri Shchekochikhin described the comments from the authorities this way:

B. K. Pugo, not yet confirmed as Soviet minister of the interior, could not quite explain to the deputies what this all-powerful 'committee of national salvation' was that could bring tanks out on the streets of Vilnius, and Defense Minister D. T. Yazov's explanation elicited nothing but stupor. Saying that he did not know all the details (since he "was not at the scene") and had not given any order for a tank and paratrooper attack, he proposed his own version of the Vilnius tragedy. It consists of the following: when the members of the "committee of national salvation" beaten by the parliament, came to the chief of the Vilnius garrison, their appearance upset the general so much that he gave orders to take over the television center, which kept broadcasting "anti-Soviet programs." That is, according to Marshal Yazov, the bloody tragedy at the television center was caused by the emotional outburst of an individual general! …

12 M. Sokolov, "Lithuania: Shevardnadze, by the Way, Warned Us …," Kommersant, 14 January 1991.

13 Yu. Shchekochikhin, "Uncontrollable Army?" Literaturnaya gazeta, 16 January 1991.

14 M. Sokolov, "The Lithuanian Crisis: Now Everything Depends on Russia," Kommersant, 21 January 1991.

If the tragedy in Vilnius was caused by the actions of one general, they can be seen as homemade mutiny, for which—as in every civilized society—the officer must be punished by law.[15]

At that time, one of Gorbachev's closest people, his aide Alexander Chernyaev, wrote to him about his view of the events:

This time the choice is: either you say directly that you will not tolerate the loss of a foot of land from the Soviet Union and you will use every means, including tanks, to keep it from happening. Or you admit that a tragic event uncontrolled from the center has occurred, that you condemn those who used force and killed people and you demand they be held responsible. In the first case, it would mean that you are burying everything you have said and done over the last five years. You admit that you yourself and the nation are not ready for a revolutionary turn onto the civilized path and that you will have to carry on and deal with the people in the old way. In the second case, you might still be able to fix things in the name of continuing the perestroika course. Although something irreversible has already occurred.[16]

Economic reality hindered an increase in repressions. In order to feed the city, grain had to be imported. In order to keep the factories going, imported parts had to be delivered. Yet there was no hard currency. The chances were slim that the USSR would get state loans from the West if it went back to a harder line.

Hence the next crossroads: continue hardening the political regime and give up all reforms or return to the path of political reforms as it had been defined in the summer of 1990?

Gorbachev chose the latter in spring 1991. His closest associates—Valentin Pavlov, chairman of the Council of Ministers of the Soviet Union; Vladimir Kryuchkov, chairman of the KGB; Oleg Baklanov, first deputy chairman of the Defense Council of the Soviet Union; Boris Pugo, minister of the interior; Vasily Starodubtsev, chairman of the Peasant Union of the Soviet Union; Alexander Tizyakov, president of the Association of State Enterprises and Industry, Construction, Transport, and Communications of the Soviet Union; Dmitri Yazov, Minister of Defense of the Soviet Union; and Gennady Yanayev, vice president of the Soviet Union—chose the former.

The culmination of events around this crossroads came between 19 and 21 August 1991. Today many commentators call the putsch operetta-like, with no chances of success. But is that so? The organizers had troops, weapons, and special forces at their command. Two years earlier, the Chinese leadership had ruthlessly crushed a mass demonstration in Beijing, with significant bloodshed.

---

15 Shchekochikhin, "Uncontrollable Army?"

16 Report by A. S. Chernyaev dated 15 January 1991, Gorbachev Foundation, Arch. No. 8780.

It did not matter that Russian history showed that this could not happen in Moscow. This was a real crossroads. Could the authorities find a reliable regiment ready to obey orders and use tanks and cannon against those who had gathered outside the White House on the night of 20 August 1991? No one knew the answer. That kind of regiment was not found, the crossroads was passed, and the Communist regime collapsed.

The country then faced yet another historical crossroads: what was to be done with the republican administrations after the disappearance of the central authorities of the world superpower—try to form a new union center or allow each republic to go its own way?

The elite of all the former union republics confidently chose independence. A few days after the failure of the GKChP, the majority of the republics declared their independence. Ukraine declared its independence on 24 August 1991. Russia recognized the independence of Lithuania, Latvia, and Estonia then, too. On 27 August Moldavia announced its sovereignty; Azerbaijan did so on 30 August, followed by Armenia, Uzbekistan, and Kirgizia.[17]

On 28 August, the Presidium of the Supreme Soviet of Ukraine promulgated its decree on subordinating military commissariats on the territory of Ukraine to the republic's Ministry of Defense.[18] The chairman of the Supreme Soviet of Ukraine, Leonid Kravchuk, called in the commanders of all military okrugs located in Ukraine and told them than now they were subordinated to Ukrainian authorities. Ukraine took over the border guards on its territory. There were no customs borders between Russia and Ukraine, Russia and Belorussia, or Russia and Kazakhstan, and it was impossible to create one along the entire expanse in a short time. Similar issues existed in the Baltics.

Without the consent of Gosbank, the central banks of the former union republics printed non-cash money, which was easily converted to cash. The union budget was almost completely without tax revenues. After the events of August 1991, the union leadership had no troops to obey its orders. Such a state cannot exist. Gorbachev and the leaders of the union republic announced that in the new situation the union authorities could no longer function. The Congress of People's Deputies of the Soviet Union dissolved itself.[19]

---

17 Izvestia, 26 August–2 September 1991.

18 Izvestia, 29 August 1991.

19 "On 2 September, in the name of the president of the USSR and leaders of ten union republics (Azerbaijan, Armenia, Belorussia, Kazakhstan, Kirgizia, Russia, Uzbekistan, Ukraine, Tajikistan, and Turkmenia), President of Kazakhstan Nazarbyaev promulgated the declaration: dissolve the union and on a parity basis form structures for the transitional period. The Congress was expected to do only one thing: confirm the constitutional act defining the structure of transitional agencies of the union—and peacefully dissolve itself." M. Sokolov, "The Union of Free Republics Is Falling Apart ...," Kommersant, 9 September 1991.

Even though the republics were quite definite on their independence, there was a choice: try to preserve some form of the no longer extant Soviet union through compromise, or legally dissolve it.

The background for this issue was the worsening economic crisis. The country had no grain and no hard currency with which to purchase it.[20] The grain situation was getting more intense. V. Akulinin, first deputy chairman of the Committee on Food Purchasing, wrote on 6 September 1991 to the chairman of the Committee on Operative Management of the Economy, Ivan Silayev, and his deputy, Yuri Luzhkov: "In order to stimulate the provision of grain and vegetable oil in state resources for 1991 the practice of purchasing it in freely convertible currency has been extended. However, the means for these purchases have not been considered."[21]

He wrote again on 27 September 1991: "Esteemed Ivan Stepanovich! Goskomprod USSR informed you earlier about the critical situation involving resources of edible wheat at the flour mill factories … At the present time, because of unsatisfactory deliveries of imported grain, the situation with bread products may deteriorate rapidly … In connection with this, we ask you to task the Ministry of the Economy USSR, MVES USSR, and Vneshekonombank USSS: take measures to deliver on the account of established credits in September-October no less than 1.2 million tons of wheat; to not delay in finding hard currency sources and buy abroad an additional 1 million tons of wheat to be delivered by 1 November 1991."[22]

---

20 Wrote Leonid Abalkin, former deputy chairman of the union government, wrote: "In early October [1991—Ye. G.], while in the USA, I met with Mr. Greenspan, head of the Federal Reserve System, one of the most experienced financial experts in modern times. We have known each other a long time, we understand each other, and practically spoke the same language. He asked me, 'Do you realize that you have only a few weeks to prevent a financial collapse?' I replied that our calculations made it two months. But in fact, the only difference lay in how we expressed the thought: a few weeks or two months is practically the same thing." See L. I. Abalkin, K tseli cherez krizis. Spustia god … [To the goal through a crisis: a year later …] (Moscow: Luch, 1992), 176. From the notes of Georgy Shakhnazarov on the meeting of the State Council on 16 October 1991: "Grigory Yavlinsky reporting on the economic union at a meeting of the State Council. He gives figures: decline of production in 1991 by 15 percent, in 1992 they expect 23–25 percent.… The end of production and price growth at 2–3 times create a dead-end situation." See G. S. Shakhnazarov, S vozhdiami i bez nikh [With leaders and without them] (Moscow: Vagrius, 2001), 482.

21 V. I. Akulinin, first deputy chairman of the Committee on Food Purchasing, to Comrade I. S. Silayev at the Committee on Operative Management of the Economy, "On Purchases of Grain with Freely Convertible Currency," 28 August 1991, GARF, f. 5446, op. 163, D. 1438, L. 57.

22 V. I. Akulinin, first deputy chairman of the Committee on Food Purchasing, to Comrade I. S. Silayev at the Committee on Operative Management of the Economy, "On Volume of Import of Wheat and Purchases of Soybeans," 27 September 1991, GARF, f. 5446, op. 163, D. 1439, L. 75.

First option: among states that had declared themselves independent, preserving the union without instruments of enforcement involved a long search for agreement on issues where their interests clashed. In a condition of increasing economic crisis, this strategy was dangerous and unrealistic.

Second option: recognizing the fait accompli. If the Soviet Union no longer existed and Russia was unable to restore it by force, then the union should be allowed to dissolve peacefully and Russia should concentrate its efforts on the creation of Russian statehood. This was the decision taken in Belovezh and then confirmed by a larger group of participants in Alma-Ata on 21 December 1991.[23]

One more dangerous crossroads was faced by those involved in negotiations on this agreement: should they reexamine the question of borders among states that had declared their independence?

There was a discussion on this issue during the negotiations in Belovezh. Boris Yeltsin and Leonid Kravchuk talked about the possibility of moving the Crimea question outside the framework of the accords and returning to it later. This was unacceptable to the Ukrainian side. Kravchuk, who had just won the presidential election, could not discuss questions of Ukraine's territorial integrity.

The people who were making the decisions remembered what had happened in Yugoslavia. They understood that reexamining the borders now, however unreasonable they might be, would precipitate an immediate crisis and set the region on the road to war. They understood equally well that preserving the ex-

---

23 Excerpt from Yegor Gaidar's speech at the meeting of the heads of the member states of the Commonwealth of Independent States: "Esteemed colleagues! For my speech, a few words on the mechanism of coordination on our work. As we agreed in Alma-Ata, especially on the proposal of the delegation from Ukraine, our Commonwealth is not a state nor on a state level. If we try to bring all questions, the level of coordination on all issues to a single level, acceptable for all republics, we will simply never come to an agreement on anything, I fear this very much. It seems to me that we must approach concordance of our policies in the maximally flexible way. If some can go for a tighter integration and stricter coordination of economic policy in various spheres, we will be able sign more binding agreements.

"The logic is as follows. Today we are unable to guarantee the stability of goods within the traditional system of limits, funds, work orders, and state orders because of the limits on managing, at the very least, the economy on the territory of Russia. In the republics they are partially more manageable, but in Russia, because of the size of its territory, the soft method—when you can make enterprises do what you think necessary without bringing things to the formal directive state order—works very poorly. Hence in Russia there an tendencies of local regionalization, the formation of customs on the level of territories, on the level of oblasts, krais, which are very dangerous and could paralyze our ability to implement any kind of economic policy, including executing any obligations that we form with you." Transcript of working session of heads of states of the Commonwealth of Independent States. 24 December 1991, GARF, f. A-259, op. 1, D. 5386, 24.12.1001, L. 1–79.

isting vague borders among republics (borders that in some cases were the product of a single man's whim) would result in serious problems in the longer term, making millions of Russian citizens national minorities in countries where they had lived for decades. However, in a country with nuclear weapons, a civil war along the lines of the Yugoslav scenario would have cost Russia, and the world, much more dearly.

The essence of the compromise, which was not written down on paper but was fully realized, was simple: We will make no territorial pretensions, recognizing the existing borders of the former union republics and raising no questions about north Kazakhstan or eastern Ukraine. In return, our partners will give Russia the nuclear weapons on their territory. This did not happen right away, but with additional efforts and the help of the United States, which was not interested in seeing the appearance of new nuclear states, the compromise was realized by fall 1996.

The accords achieved in Belorussia on 8 December 1991 and confirmed on 21 December in Alma-Ata made it possible to sign the agreement on strategic nuclear arms on 20 December. It fixed the obligations of the participating states to help in the liquidation of nuclear arms in Ukraine, Belorussia, and Kazakhstan, and established that by 1 July 1992 these republics would guarantee the removal of tactical nuclear weapons to central bases for their dismantling under joint supervision. It was agreed that the parties saw no obstacles to moving nuclear arms from the territory of Belorussia, Kazakhstan, and Ukraine to the territory of the RSFSR.[24]

---

24 Agreement on joint measures in regard to nuclear weapons. (See Resolution of the Supreme Soviet RSFSR, "On Ratification of the Agreement on the Creations of the Commonwealth of Independent States," 12 December 1991, No. 2014-1.) On the removal of tactical nuclear weapons by 1 June 1992 to central bases for their dismantlement under joint supervision, see V. F. Davydov, "Raspad SSSR i nerasprostranenie iadernogo oruzhiia [Disintegration of the USSR and non-proliferation of nuclear weapons]," SShA: ekonomika, politika, ideologiia, 1992, no. 1: 265. On the concerns of Western analysts, which often turned into plain hysteria, over the fate of Russian tactical nuclear weapons in case the Soviet Union collapsed, see G. Milhollen and D. White, "Razval sovetskoi iadernoi moshchi—blago ili ugroza? [The collapse of soviet nuclear power—good or threat?]," Mezhdunarodnaia zhizn', 1992, no. 1: 43–55.

1992–1993

In December 1991 the Supreme Soviet of the RSFSR supported the dissolution of the USSR.[25] This was a precondition for stabilizing the situation and avoiding the threat of civil war, but it did not solve the fundamental economic problems. The country was still bankrupt, with its hard currency reserves near zero. It was bad enough that the country not buy grain, but there were no funds to pay the freight for delivery by ship of the grain received on foreign state credits. Optimistic estimates put the grain reserves at lasting until February or March 1992.[26]

Thus the Russian leadership faced a most important historical crossroads: Should they force delivery of food to the cities by taking away grain from the kolkhozes and retaining state prices? Or, on the contrary, should they encourage food to flow to the cities by liberalizing prices and making selling to the state profitable for the kolkhozes?

---

25 On 12 December 1991, Russia left the USSR, denouncing the Union agreement of 1922 by decision of its parliament. The results of the vote were: pro, 161 (65.2 %); against, 3 (1.2 %); abstained, 9 (3.6 %); voted, 173 (70 %). Bulletin No. 21 of the joint sessions of the Soviet of the Republics and the Soviet of Nationalities, IV session of the Supreme Soviet RSFSR, 12 December 1991. On 26 December the Soviet Republics, one of the chambers of the Supreme Soviet, met for the last time at the Kremlin and passed the declaration declaring the end of the existence of the USSR as a state and as a subject of international law, No. 142-N.

26 "The country in the nearest future may experience an emergency situation with delivery of bread supplies to residents and of concentrated feed to farms. Around 8 million tons of food and feed grains are spent monthly for these needs. Specialists asses the remaining state resources (not counting seeds) at 13 million tons as of 1 March of this year, and almost half is located in the Kazakh SSR. This means that supplies of food grain (except in Kazakhstan, where there is enough until the new harvest) will be exhausted by the end of March. Today we are already experiencing an extremely worrying situation with flour supplies. At the necessary norms for 30 days, the flour supply in Azerbaijan and Armenian SSR is 6 days, in Georgian SSR—7 days, Tadjik SSR—8, Moldova and Kirgiz SSR—9. The supplies of flour will last fewer than 10 days in Moscow, the oblasts of Ivanov, Tula, Nizhny Nonvgorod, Tyumen, Sverdlovsk, Chita, Kamchatka, and a few other oblasts.

"The imported grain is not a solution for the bread problem. In January–March of this year, only 3.7 million tons of imported grain was delivered, when 12.4 million tons was expected. Repeated calls from the country's leadership to increase delivery of grain from the Kazakh SSR and also for an accelerated delivery by important have made no tangible changes on the situation." V. Akulinin, Department of Agro-industry, to Comrade V. S. Pavlov, "On the Possibility of an Emergency Situation in Supplying the Populace with Bread Products and Cattle Breeders with Concentrated Feeds," 18 March 1991, GARF, f. 5446, op. 164, D. 560, L. 16.

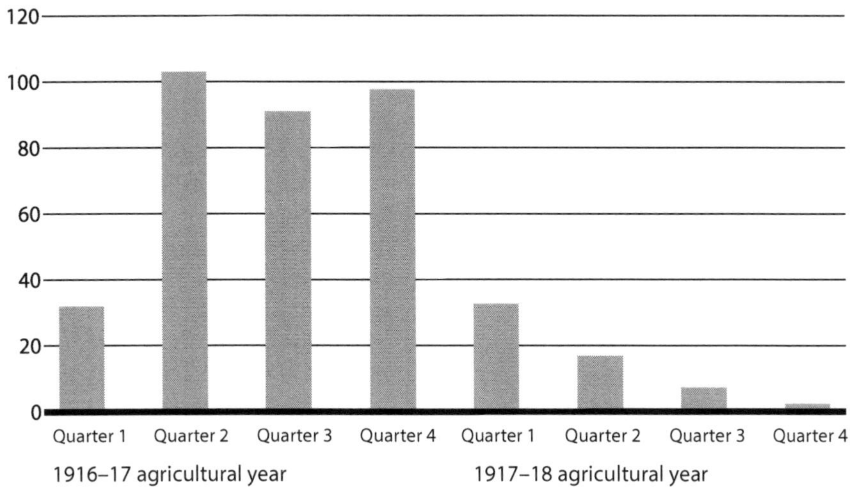

Figure 11. Actual supplies of grain, 1916–18 (millions of poods)
Source: A. Sviderskii, Chetyre goda prodovol'stvennoi raboty. Stat'i i otchetnye materialy [Four years of food work. Articles and reports] (Moscow: Gosudarstvennoe izdatel'stvo, 1922), 130

Taking grain by force meant following the path chosen by the tsarist government in 1915–16 during an acute crisis of food supplies for cities and the army. This path was continued by the Provisional Government and then with greater cruelty by the Bolshevik government. This was the path of requisitioning, which V. I. Lenin called "the heroic campaign for grain with machine guns."[27] The results are known: they did not manage to take away the grain (Figure 11).

Choosing that path in 1991–92, lacking reliable troops and not having a clear idea of whom the militia would support in the regions where grain was being taken, was risky. It was not even discussed seriously. The difference in the intellectual atmosphere predominating in the 1910s and in the 1990s played its role. In the 1910s the concept of the salutary effect of state regulation of the economy was an article of faith. To understand this, it is enough to read the tsarist, Provisional, and Bolshevik governments' documents on food production. In the 1990s, when the danger of statist experiments in the economy was obvious, faith in the wisdom of such attempts had dwindled.

Since the grain supply in major cities would last until February or March, the grain harvest in Russia would begin in July, and there was no hard currency to buy food abroad, the only solution was to offer a price the sellers would

27 V. I. Lenin, Complete Collected Works, 5th ed. (Moscow: Izdatel'stvo politicheskoi literatury, 1962), 50:85.

consider acceptable. And that meant taking a different path, the path of price liberalization, which Lenin followed in spring 1921, when he faced a political crisis caused by the paralysis in food distribution for cities.

The Russian leadership approached the question of price liberalization at a time when a significant portion of the population rejected the very idea of moving to free prices, there was an expectation of famine, and dissatisfaction was growing. Getting through this historic crossroads was politically difficult but necessary. However, the technical aspect of working out a solution that averted famine by liberalizing prices in the post-Soviet space was not simple. The Soviet monetary system differed from the system in market economies, as it was based on so-called interbranch exchanges. In the USSR it did not matter which institution of the all-Union banking system gave credits or got them. The mutual obligations could be clarified by year's end in order to amortize the accumulated debt. This system can work only under harsh political control, when it would never occur to the head of a central bank in the Union or the autonomous republics to give credits to Union republics or oblasts without consulting with Gosbank USSR and keeping within the limits it set. Maintaining this system under conditions of political liberalization and economic crisis was impossible. The republics' central banks ignored the directions from Gosbank USSR, giving loans to republic governments and large enterprises that were able to lobby for them.[28]

Similar example are known in economic history. The most characteristic is what happened after the collapse of the Austro-Hungarian Empire.[29] Hyperinflation occurred in Hungary and Austria. Only Czechoslovakia avoided it by introducing its own currency. But at that time there were only three countries involved. There were fifteen in the post-Soviet space. In that situation it was profitable for the small republics in a single ruble zone to increase monetary emissions. This meant that the greatest danger in keeping a single monetary system was to Russia (Figure 12).

Figure 13 shows how accounts were kept among former Union republics as of summer 1992.

---

28 From the reply of V. Solovov, then deputy chairman of the Central Bank, RSFSR, to F. Lukashov, people's deputy, Russian Federation: "In connection with your query to Vice Premier of the Government of the Russian Federation V. F. Shumeiko, at his request, the Central Bank of the Russian Federation states that there was no permission from the competent organs of the Russian Federation for Ukraine to undertake large-scale emission of rubles. After the Central Bank of the Russian Federation learned of the credit emission made by the national bank of Ukraine, commensurate measures were taken to protect the interests of Russia's monetary system from the consequences of this emission; in particular, on 1 July we introduced a regimen of interbank accounting, which does not allow unlimited rubles from Ukraine into the accounts of banks of the Russian Federation." (Arkhiv TsB. D. 5136. 10.10.1992. L. 40).

29 R. Dornbusch, Post-Communist Monetary Problems: Lessons from the End of the Austro-Hungarian Empire (San Francisco: Institute for Contemporary Studies, 1994).

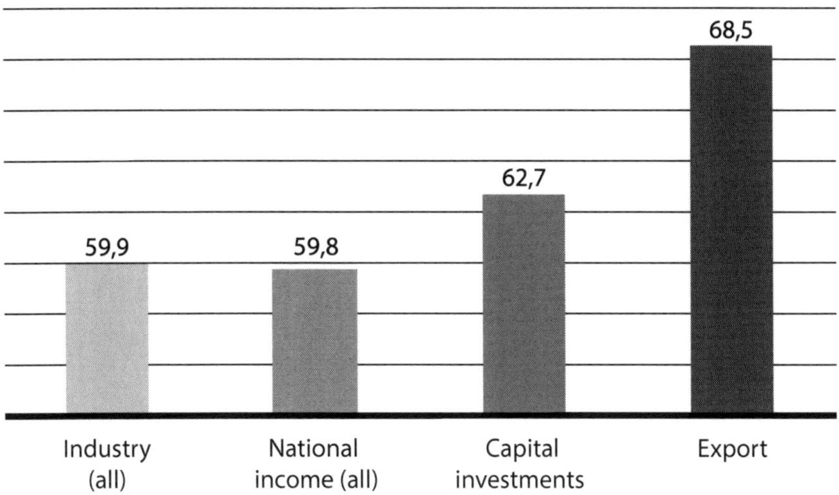

Figure 12. Russia's share of the USSR's industrial production, national income, capital investments, and exports, 1990 (percent)

Source: Narodnoe khoziaistvo RSFSR v 1990 godu. Stat. ezhegodnik (Moscow: Respublikanskii informationno-izdatel'skii tsentr, 1991); Narodnoe khoziaistvo SSR v 1990. Stat. ezhegodnik (Moscow: Finansy i statistika, 1991)

The system of money circulation, like the banking system, cannot be changed overnight. But it is also impossible to explain to people that there won't be any bread from February or March 1992 until July 1992.

This led to yet another crossroads: liberalize prices without reliable controls over money circulation, or put off the liberalization question until a Russian national currency could be introduced?

This was the subject of discussion in the fall of 1991. Any of the choices meant risk and no guarantee of success. The first option proposed and discussed at a meeting of the Russian government in early November 1991 was to conduct a partial liberalization of prices starting in January 1992, which would allow the economy to adapt gradually to the changed reality, and on 1 July 1992 to introduce a Russian national currency, transfer the relations with the central banks of states that had declared their independence to correspondent accounts, liberalize prices, and introduce ruble convertibility for current operations.[30]

But just two weeks later, after an analysis of the state of food delivery, we came to the conclusion that this option was impossible.[31] The food crisis was

30 Yegor Gaidar's speech at the meeting of the government of the RSFSR on 15 November 1991. "Stenogramma zasedaniiia Pravitel'stva RSFSR 15 noiabria 1991 goda," GARF, f. A-259, op. 1, D. 5383, 1991, L. 6–13.

31 Yuri Luzhkov reported in November 1991: "The government of Moscow brings to your attention the fact that food supplies for the population remain critical. … Because

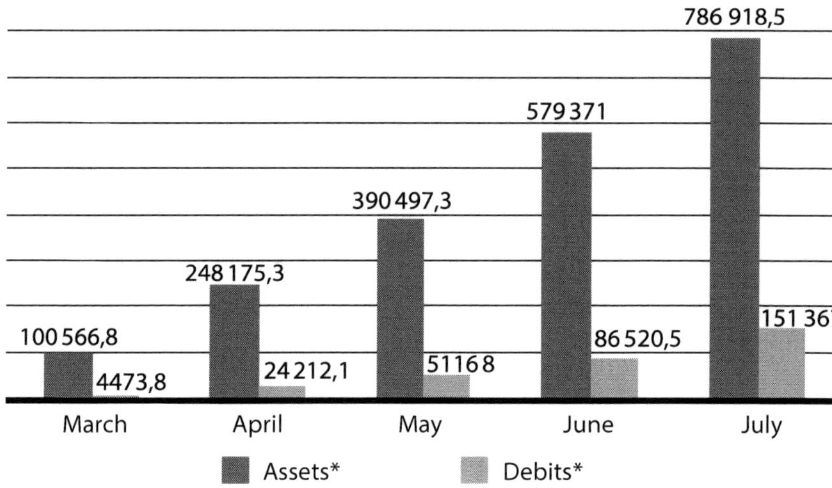

Figure 13. Remaining accounts of CIS countries, March–July 1992 (data from consolidated balance sheet; millions of rubles on the first of the month)

Assets are the combined property rights belonging to a juridical person in the form of fixed assets, nonmaterial assets, financial deposits, and financial demands toward other juridical persons. Debits are the combined debts of the juridical person. They include own capital (authorized capital stock and share capital) as well as borrowed capital (credits, loans), grouped by contents and due dates.

Note. As of I July 1992 there were 1,327 RCCs [Settlement Centers of the Central Bank of Russia], which had 3,698 subaccounts and correspondent accounts with all banks in the Russian Federation.

Source: Spravki o sostoianii raschetov, Arkhiv Tsentrobanka, D. 5343, August 1992, L. 43–48

too profound—there was no chance of avoiding hunger and the concomitant cataclysms before the new harvest. That is when the decision was made to implement full-scale price liberalization.

In implementing the decree on price liberalization, the government came up against legal barriers and the particular mentality of Soviet citizens. Private or any other trade activity unsanctioned by the state in the Soviet period was considered entrepreneurial and was punished harshly by the RSFSR's criminal

---

of a shortage of 40,000 tons of resources and the cessation of delivieries of animal fat from Ukraine, Estonia, Latvia, and Moldova, it is sold only periodically, and there are no remains of animal fats. By a union contract 20,000 tons of animal fats has been bought as import. The entire purchase must be sent to Moscow. ... Moscow may end up without food in January 1992." Yu. M. Luzhkov, head of Moscow Government, to G. E. Burbulis, first deputy chairman of RSFSR Government, GARF, f. 410, op. 1, D. 4818, 22.11.1991 , L. 197–98. Information from Chita Oblast: "Flour ration 260 grams per person. That is below wartime quotas, the situation with bread is critical." V. Tikhon'kikh, chairman of the Baleisky Regional Soviet of People's Deputies, to B. N. Yeltsin, president of the RSFSR, and I. S. Silayev, chairman of the Council of Ministers RSFSR, GARF. f. 527, op. 7, D. 9134, 09.08.1991, L. 320.

code. Many years of propaganda had instilled the idea that trade was speculation, and so any extra goods both at enterprises and at home beyond what a family needed for itself were not sent to market, even though that would have eased the acuteness of the food shortage The food products brought by kolkhoz farmers from the villages were difficult to sell in cities.

In these conditions, a group of Leningrad deputies led by Petr Filippov and M. Kiselev prepared a presidential decree, which was signed by Yeltsin on 29 January 1992. The decree, "On Freedom of Trade," had an enormous influence on the development of market relations in Russia. It allowed millions of Russians to get through the difficult years of reform by getting involved in trade and intermediary work within the country and in imports from abroad. The choice to accelerate liberalization and force the lifting of limitations on trade prevented a catastrophe in the food market in spring 1992. However, with control over money emissions destroyed, a very high price had to be paid.

One of the crossroads of the period involved the order of the reforms: privatization first, followed by price liberalization, or vice versa?

It is obvious that an effectively functioning market presupposes a large sector of private property. It is also clear that private property is not very effective without a market. This is the story of the chicken and the egg: which should come first? In Russia the choice was made to start with price liberalization, then create market mechanisms for integration into the global market, and subsequently transition to a convertible ruble; only then would there be full-scale privatization.

Price liberalization is a difficult choice politically but easily executed technically. Its necessity was dictated by the realities of food supplies in late 1991 and early 1992. Privatization is a technically complex process, requiring the creation of a legislative base and the subsequent elaboration of hundreds of normative acts and concrete decisions for thousands of enterprises involving millions of employees. Therefore, even just from the technical point of view, liberalizing prices after privatization would have meant putting it off for two or three years, which was unacceptable for food distribution in the country.

The Soviet reality of the late 1980s and early 1990s was that the bureaucrats, that is, the nomenklatura, were the ones who were most interested in privatization. This social group was the first to understand the prospects and advantages of private property. And since they were holding the real levers of power, they began using them to acquire property. This phenomenon came to be known as "spontaneous" or "nomenklatura privatization."

Nomenklatura privatization used various financial and legal technologies, the most "honest" of which was rent with purchase. The director of a large enterprise, as a private individual, established a society with a founding capital of a couple of hundred rubles and rented the enterprise assets to it, with the right to purchase the enterprise at its balance price, that is, for kopeks. The purchase was formulated in strict accordance with the society agreement and existing laws.

The government faced the urgent task of bringing illegal and uncontrollable privatization into a civilized framework. One consideration was that only the methods of privatization that fit the existing distribution of political forces and corresponded to the balance of interests of various social groups could be instituted. The administrative ability to coerce obedience to normative acts passed by the federal government was close to zero, so passing decrees and resolutions that were right in principle but would not be followed was not the way. Rather, a realizable concept of privatization had to be constructed that did not lose sight of the main goal—forming the institution of private property in Russia.

Thus at each crossroads along the way to privatization, we had to remember that, on one hand, uncontrollable privatization by the nomenklatura was already in full swing by early 1992 and, on the other hand, the government's ability to affect the situation was extremely limited. This meant that the real options for privatization were extremely limited. Unfortunately, this simple truth has not been taken into account in most of the subsequent discussions about privatization.

The most important crossroads at that time was the choice between mass free privatization and privatization for money.

Vitali Naishul had proposed the concept of free voucher privatization back in 1987. The authors of this book thought it too simple to be able to solve an extremely complex problem. In 1987 we criticized the concept for making no distinction between the giants of chemical industry, food factories, and oil production enterprises, not taking into account the real condition of basic funds, and therefore inevitably resulting in millions of people being hurt or dissatisfied.

Privatization for money, in comparison, had inarguable advantages. It not only made the transfer of enterprises into the hands of efficient owners quicker but also helped to reduce the state budget deficit. The monies received could be used to pay the salaries of state-supported professionals and to help needy strata. Using these arguments, it took only two months from when the new government came into power to form the necessary legislative base and launch money privatization, starting in 1992 with retail trade and enterprises involved in consumer services. Only a small part of state and municipal property could be realized through this more consistent and effective privatization scheme. Despite the powerful resistance of the elite of Soviet trade on the federal level and in the regions, the program was implemented completely.

But by spring 1992 it was clear that given the historical conditions, privatization for money in large industry, while more effective, did not fit the political window of opportunity. This "big privatization" could be implemented only as free voucher privatization. The simplest argument boiled down to the fact that citizens did not have the money equivalent to the total value of all the state property. We had to take the political limitations into account as well—the Supreme Soviet RSFSR kept moving toward the Communist positions, and the idea of free privatization was popular.

The principle of free division of state property among all Russians was already enshrined in the laws "On Privatization of State and Municipal Enterprises in the RSFSR" and "On Personal Privatization Accounts," passed in July 1991 by the Supreme Soviet RSFSR on the proposal of Petr Filippov, the chairman of the subcommittee on privatization. The Russian parliament elected in the first free alternative elections reflected the mood of the electorate. Perhaps that is why even among its "democratic" elements, free privatization was popular. As well, the Communist and industrial fractions supported voucher privatization at that time.

Therefore, the historic crossroads on privatization looked like this in the summer of 1992: either free privatization regulated by law or the loss of the state's control over the unfolding nomenklatura privatization.

This was the logic of the major privatization that began in fall 1992 with a mass transformation of medium and large state enterprises into stock societies and the sale of their stocks as personal property in exchange for a specially created form of payment—privatization checks (vouchers).

It would have been unrealistic to expect enterprises to pass into the hands of efficient owners right away in the course of free privatization. But there were solutions built into the process that would lead to this sooner or later. And it did in fact happen: today there are almost no owners left who cannot manage their assets themselves, or who do not bring in professionals to do it.

In order to ensure this result, it was incredibly important to get through two crossroads properly. The first crossroads held this choice: cash privatization checks (vouchers) or non-cash named privatization accounts (deposits).

The privatization legislation of 1991 called for every citizen of the country to have a named privatization account (deposit) at Sberbank, which could not be transferred or sold. The circulation of shares acquired through the privatization deposit was limited. This construction, the result of a compromise with the left in passing the privatization laws, deprived these bank deposits of a very important quality—liquidity. This set back the appearance of effective private property owners for a long time and destroyed hopes for the birth of a stock market.

In addition, the privatization accounts (deposits) meant enormous inconvenience for people. Every resident, both those in large cities and those living in tiny villages, had to open a special bank account and then make numerous transfers in order to acquire packets of shares in enterprises under privatization. The free privatization through accounts in Sberbank was difficult organizationally and risked leading to a technical collapse that would block the entire privatization process. It was not surprising that the heads of Sberbank expressed an unwillingness to take on this vast and risky project. Entrusting privatization to a poorly managed and complex state institution with no incentive to implement it would have been absurd.

Therefore, by the president's decree of 14 August 1992, instead of accounts at Sberbank, privatization vouchers in document form were prepared for distribution to every citizen in the land. Those people who did not want to transfer their portion of state property into shares could sell the vouchers on the market. Broadly put, this created a demand for shares of the enterprises being privatized and laid the foundation for the establishment of stock market institutions. The privatization checks were quoted on markets, giving a strong impulse for their expansion. The voucher price was watched along with the dollar. This generated an opportunity to concentrate capital, gave rise to investment funds, and created thousands of jobs for stock market professionals. It is no accident that even today the Russian stock market is the most developed stock market in the CIS.

The second crossroads was the choice between the property of labor collectives and the property of members of labor collectives.

It involved strategic risk. The demand to implement privatization in favor of labor collectives was popular. It was supported by union and councils of labor collectives, and behind them were the enterprise directors. Without their support, it would not be possible to have privatization, but the task was to meet this demand yet not create a cooperative market socialism to replace Soviet socialism.

It must be borne in mind that at the time of the 11 June 1992 confirmation of the Privatization Program, the Supreme Soviet had moved considerably left. The government concession was the second version of privatization, with a transfer of 51 percent of shares to the labor collective. However, in exchange, the government got a concession as well—the shares were transferred not to the labor collectives but to the members of the collectives. The crossroads had been negotiated the right way, and the law established one of the root differences between capitalism and market socialism.

As a result, a number of approaches to privatization were used in the course of the mass free privatization, each of which politically balanced potentially explosive social groups, from directors to members of labor collectives and pensioners. Of course, it would not be correct to say that each group was satisfied; rather, each was equally dissatisfied. However, this achieved a balance of power that legitimized the right to property for all interested strata, preserved their interests by utilizing a variety of approaches to privatization, and launched the process of privatization. The numerous necessary compromises did not undermine the strategic goal, which was the creation of the institution of private property in Russia.

The big voucher privatization began in accordance with the presidential decree of 14 August 1992. In November and December of that year the first vouch-

Table 2

Basic indicators of privatization in Russia, 1992–95

Cumulative results from 1 Jan 1992	1 Jan 1993	1 Jan 1994	1 Jan 1995
State enterprises on independent balance, units	204,998	156,635	126,846
Applications made, units	102,330	125,492	143,968
Applications denied, units	5,390	9,985	12,317
Realized applications, units	46,815	88,577	112,625
Sale price (billions of rubles, old prices)	57	752	1,867
Value of property in realized applications (billions of rubles, old prices)	193	653	1,092
State enterprises turned into a stock company (shares sold on market), units	2,376	14,073	24,048
Enterprises rented, units	22,216	20,886	16,826
Including rented with purchase, units	13,868	14,978	12,806

Sources: Ministry of State Property, Russian Fund of Federal Property

er auctions were held and state enterprises started to be auctioned off. A stock market was forming gradually. This laid the foundation for further redistribution of property by market methods.

At this time as well, the Supreme Soviet RSFSR, completely pro-Communist by then, began its continuing struggle against privatization. Privatization was almost stopped in spring 1993 as a result of the confrontation between the president and the Supreme Soviet. A critical clash was avoided because of popular support for Yeltsin and his reforms in the 25 April referendum. The people supported the reforms at the referendum, but on 1 May demonstrations by opponents in Moscow ended in bloodshed. This showed how hard the economic, social, and psychological burden of change had been for much of the population. Subsequently, the fierce struggle within the government put a brake on privatization and put it on the brink of being repealed several times. However, by the middle of 1994 this historical crossroads had been traversed: the program of free privatization on the basis of vouchers was completed.

Along with examples of the right road taken in privatization, we can point to examples of serious errors. One was made in the discussion of the problem of participation by citizens who had no competence in this sphere (the "babushka" problem). Some discussants maintained that an intermediary should be created for them, a professional institution, the voucher investment funds (ChIF). The idea was that a diligent elaboration of the ChIF base would help those who did not want to sell their vouchers but were unable to evaluate the pros and cons of

Table 3

Comparison of the integral efficiency of state and privatized enterprises in 1995, by industry

Industry	Integrated efficiency		
	State enterprises	Stock companies with state portion	
		Above 25 %	Below 25 %
Black metallurgy	0.384	0.644	0.505
Color metallurgy	0.534	0.259	0.726
Chemical industry	0.309	0.533	0.895
Machine building	0.128	0.696	0.922
Construction materials	0.178	0.807	0.775
Light industry	0.292	0.461	0.681
Food industry	0.229	0.488	0.852
Medical industry	0.288	N/A	0.727

Note: The selection comprised 2,438 enterprises on the basis of the Goskomstat Register, including 575 state enterprises, 596 privatized enterprises with a state portion of more than 25 percent, and 1,267 privatized enterprises with a state portion of less than 25 percent. The integrated indicator of efficiency is calculated on the basis of four indicators of economic efficiency (productivity, return, yield on capital investments, and working capital turnover) and four indicators of financial condition (coefficients of autonomy, maneuverability, availability of own circulating assets, and current liquidity). The integrated indicator was calculated for each group of enterprises and evaluated the given group on a complex of characteristics. The integrated indicator represents a level of characteristics (individual indicators) achieved by the group. The level of each individual indicator is normalized with the compared groups of enterprises from 0 to 1: 0 is the worst average indicator, 1 the best.
Source: Leontyev Center, 1996

acquiring shares of various enterprises. The opponents of this idea considered it excessive and unrealizable. We chose the first option, as a result of which businessmen instituted several hundred ChIFs, which gathered up more than forty million checks. But the voucher investment fund project totally collapsed, due to unprofessional managers and outright theft. In effect, all forty million investors were deceived. This failure was a tremendous factor in the development of a general negative attitude toward privatization. Today it is clear that in order to have real control over the ChIFs we would have needed to build a system that was comparable in complexity and influence to bank supervision, which, as we know, was established in Russia only by the end of the 1990s. To create such a system in 1992–93 was simply impossible.

Despite the serious mistakes made, major privatization became irreversible and picked up speed (Table 2).

As we have said, the process of forming effective property owners takes time; however, even at this early stage, many enterprises found diligent owners. The statistics presented in Table 3 show that in Russia, as in other countries, private enterprises are more efficient than state enterprises. However, the data demonstrate only the first signs of private property's positive effect on the efficiency of production and do not yet speak of the true victory of private property in Russia.

1994–1996

This period, replete with complex crossroads in economic policy, was the prologue to the most important political crossroads of the 1990s, the presidential elections of 1996. A significant drop in production, lowered quality of life, and accumulated weariness with lagging reforms against a backdrop of radically changed living standards for tens of millions of people put powerful trump cards in the hands of the Communist opposition. The Communists, who controlled parliament and a great number of governors in the regions, had quickly revived after the events of October 1993 and steadily increased their resources for the coming presidential elections. The essence of the looming historic crossroads became ever clearer: continued movement on the road to building a market economy and democracy, or a return to the Communist path?

We can use the two most eventful spheres, macroeconomic policy and privatization with mortgage auctions, to characterize the period's economic policy.

The ruble collapsed on 11 October 1994. In one day the dollar rose from 2,833 to 3,996 rubles. This event, which subsequently came to be known as Black Tuesday, created a real political shock, with dramatic political and economic consequences. The chairman of the Central Bank, Viktor Gerashchenko, and the acting finance minister, Sergei Dubinin, were fired. One of the authors of this book received an unexpected proposal from the chairman of the government, Victor Chernomyrdin, to create a new economic team in the government; he accepted and on 5 November 1994 was appointed first deputy chairman of the government.

What were the causes of Black Tuesday? The Central Bank's monetary policy, not distinguished by strictness in the previous period, had become even weaker in the spring and summer of 1994. Under the influence of the agrarian lobby and the military-industrial and fuel-energy complexes, the bank saw a growing wave of credits—but those credits were essentially just unbacked monetary emissions. The weakened team of reformers in the government could not stand up to these actions, especially since most people in the Russian economic community at the time did not consider the connection between monetary policy and inflation significant, or even denied that there was one, while the leaders of the Central Bank openly proclaimed its main goal to be the giving of credits to support domestic manufacture. Bearing in mind that the budget deficit for 1994 was 10 percent of GDP, a financial and economic crash was inevitable. The banks, in trying to maximize profits, unleashed speculative attacks on the ruble in August and September, which triggered Black Tuesday.

The new economic team formed in November 1994 faced a real threat that the currency crisis would turn into a financial and economic catastrophe. The combination of the crash in the exchange rate and inflation, which had reached 16.4 percent a month by December 1994, resulted in panic on the financial markets and consistently reduced the Central Bank's reserves. In January 1995 its gross hard currency reserves had fallen to the critical amount of $1.5 billion, and its purely international reserve to $865 million. Since the Central Bank had to perform daily currency interventions in amounts greater than $100 million on some days, the risk of sovereign default was just days away.

The situation could be saved only by an immediate and radical reevaluation of the country's financial and economic policy. Given the rate of reduction in the country's hard currency reserves, there was just a bit over a month in which to elaborate a new policy, get it approved by the government and the Central Bank, obtain support from international financial organization, announce the policy, and start implementing it. The main goals of the policy were macroeconomic stabilization and reduction of inflation. Its main tenets were in a statement by the government and Central Bank, "On Economic Policy in 1995," issued on 10 March 1995 and ratified by a resolution of the Russian Federation government on 15 April 1995 (no. 334). However, the policy had been implemented immediately, starting on 1 January 1995.

The key points of the policy included:

- A ban as of 1 January 1995 on direct credits from the Central Bank to finance the deficit in the federal budget (except from certain specified cases) and on centralized credited from the government and the Central Bank to agricultural organizations
- The creation of a mechanism for financing the state budget deficit without printing money
- The revaluation of tax policy, the reduction of existing tax benefits, and a moratorium on creating new ones
- The resumption of privatization

In order to achieve these goals, we had to do the following: first, resume negotiations with international financial organizations and obtain signed agreements and credits; second, get approval from the State Duma, controlled by the Communists, for corresponding changes in the "Law on the Central Bank," as well as ratification of an unprecedentedly harsh budget; and third, overcome the growing mass strike movement (primarily in the coal industry, with its simultaneous reform).

There was no support for these measures in the democratic camp, either. Thus, Grigory Yavlinsky, leader of the Yabloko Party, stated in April 1995

Table 4

Exchange rate of the ruble, index of consumer prices, and Russia's international reserves, 1995

	Official exchange rate (at end of month, rubles for dollar)	Consumer price index	Pure international reserves (billions of dollars)
January	4048	17.8	0.865
February	4473	11.0	1.252
March	4897	8.9	1.858
April	5130	8.5	2.203
May	4995	7.9	3.964
June	4538	6.7	5.773
July	4415	5.4	6.002
August	4447	4.6	5.982
September	4508	4.5	5.657
October	4504	4.7	6.261
November	4580	4.5	5.393
December	4640	3.2	5.884

Source: Central Bank, Russian Federation

that "the institutionally inevitable level of inflation for this preparatory period is around 10 percent a month."[32] And even in December 1995, when the facts disproved this thesis, he continued to believe that "inflation is the temperature, not the disease. The disease is the monopolism of our economy, the absence of a competitive field, the inability of enterprises to win markets … If we only fight inflation fanatically … it means that we will not pull the deep roots of inflation that feed it despite all the 'macroeconomic' efforts of the government. The fight should be against not inflation but its causes."[33]

Nevertheless, the great majority of our goals were met. The classic method of "nominal anchor" was used to restore macroeconomic balance. In July, against the background of the positive conditions created in the first half of 1995, a "currency corridor" of 4,300–4,900 rubles to the dollar was introduced. Initially it was established for one quarter, until 1 October 1995.

With the introduction of the currency corridor in July, the government economic team publicly declared that if it could not be maintained for the quarter, the entire team would quit. Not only was it maintained, but with a small ex-

32 "The 'Stationary Bandit' on the Path to Stabilization," Segodnya, 22 April 1995.

33 "We Must Act with Lapidary Accuracy," Izvestiya, 15 December 1995.

pansion it was continued into the fourth quarter. This was of fundamental significance in removing uncertainty regarding changes in the exchange rate and promoting increased trust in the monetary and credit policy as a whole.

In February 1995 we reached agreement on credits from the IMF and World Bank. In March, the federal budget for 1995 was confirmed. The miners' strike that had begun in the spring of 1995 was over by the summer.

The break in the trends of inflation, exchange rate, and pure international reserves over 1995 is shown in Table 4.

The economic reforms of 1995 stimulated important strategic reforms that could not bring immediate results but had a strong influence on the country's development. Work began on the tax code and on documents relating to the reform of pensions, social insurance, health care, and education. The transition began to a treasury implementation of the budget. A long-term program for lowering the budget deficit to 3 percent was passed. A government commission began working on preparations for Russia's accession to the World Trade Organization. Significant progress was made in most of these areas. But the tasks were so complex and the resistance so powerful that many of these measures remain not fully realized today.

The economic transformations implemented in 1995 could not be painless. The first to feel the blow were commercial banks. It would be no exaggeration to say that almost the entire new banking sector of Russia was born and grew up in conditions of superhigh inflation. Inevitably, the dominant activity in such a situation is short-term banking operations oriented toward speculative results with extremely low efficiency and high costs. The banking sector was quite skeptical of the government strategy to lower inflation, and we were unable to get adequate measures to correct the strategy of commercial banks. Until 1995 Russian banks were able to compensate for unsuccessful portfolio decisions and high credit risks by never-fail operations on the currency market, an enormous percentage margin, and inflationary devaluation of all losses.

The start of stabilization demanded that bank managers first have a rational understanding of macroeconomic consequences and then change their strategy of competitive behavior. The basic mistake was an underestimation of the scale of the relative change in profitability of ruble and currency assets. Once they realized this, the economic team tried open dialogue with the banks in order to help them understand the essence and degree of seriousness of the economic maneuver under way. Speaking in May 1995 at the congress of Associations of Russian Banks, one of the authors of this book spoke about the inevitability of lowering inflation and "expressed absolute confidence in ending the era of developing banks in conditions of 15–20 percent inflation."[34] However, the banks never developed a true understanding.

34 "Congress of Associations of Russian Banks," Kommersant, 25 May 1995.

The crisis phenomena in the banking sphere began to manifest themselves by June 1995, when some banks violated the conditions of their obligations on the interbank credit market (MBK). However, the market continued functioning with its former intensity right up until 23 August, when trading was suspended for technical reasons. The majority of market makers left the market, fearing a chain of nonpayments. The daily turnover dropped from 1.14 trillion rubles to 130 billion rubles, creating a liquidity deficit. Quotes on one-day INSTAR credits rose from 77 percent at the start of the crisis to 275–350 percent in the last week of August. On some trades the price of monetary resources reached 2,000 percent annually.

This collapse of the interbank market was inevitable, since its turnover did not correspond to the real degree of credit risk. Despite dramatic consequences and even the bankruptcy of several banks, on the whole this crisis played a positive role, since it revealed which banks were ineffective and forced the Central Bank to increase regulation in 1996, paying much more attention to whether banks obeyed the norms.

An extremely hard consequence of the tightened monetary-credit and fiscal policy was the growing nonpayment of salaries (particularly painful in the state-funded sphere). This elicited justified criticism of the government and its economic team. The problem of owed salaries was not solved until after 2000, with growth of the economy and harsh measures for natural monopolies that refused imputational payment systems.

On the whole, the economic reforms of 1994–95 helped achieve significant macroeconomic stabilization, harnessed price growth, lowered inflation by 80 percent, and turned around the economic situation, from many years of falling GDP to its subsequent growth in 1997. While a high price had to be paid for financial stabilization, it laid a foundation for later solving the problems that resulted from the harsh macroeconomic policy.

* * *

In the period 1994–96 important crossroads were encountered in the privatization of state property as well. The conclusion of free privatization in mid-1994 had not yet meant a real transition of the Russian economy into the hands of private owners. Tens of thousands of stock societies were registered, and people were trading privatization checks for their shares. But in the majority of enterprises, new owners could not use their legal rights, and the corporate mechanism of subordinating the management to them and permitting management to be replaced did not work. The true owners of the enterprises were still the "red directors," who continued to live in accordance with Soviet logic. They did not care who owned the shares and assumed that they would continue to be in charge. Because they had all the advantages, the directors won the struggle between directors and shareholders.

In addition, dozens of industrial giants remained state property. They had been removed from the program of mass privatization under pressure from the directors, whose lobby in the government was very powerful in 1993–94. The oil giants, metallurgy complexes, and shipbuilding remained under the control of the directors, many of whom were members of the Communist Party and were advocates of state ownership, which essentially gave them unlimited control over the shares.

It should be remembered that in those years industry ministers were categorically opposed to the privatization of enterprises in their fields. They were supported by the "strong economist" Oleg Soskovets, the first vice premier and the number two man in terms of real political power in the country, and the siloviki Alexander Korzhakov, Mikhail Barsukov, and Anatoli Kulikov. The market economic reforms that had begun in 1992 now got held up, and there was a great chance that they would remain yet another failed attempt at transforming the economy.

In March 1995 Vladimir Potanin suggested implementing a mortgage auctions scheme. Its essence was to auction the right to mortgage large or controlling packets of shares in the largest enterprises that were still state property. The bank that won an auction for one of these enterprises had to give the government a loan. The government had eighteen months to repay the loan or turn the enterprise over to the bank. The idea, supported by Soskovets, gave hope that the market reforms could continue.

This led to a crossroads that had both economic components (passing control over major state enterprises to private hands, receiving real income for the budget) and even more important political ones. One of the realities of the times was Yeltsin's loss of popularity over the difficulties created by the reforms and by the losses in the Chechen war. We had broad support for the Communists, on one hand, and on the other a regime discredited by the terrible situation in the economy, a low standard of living, unpaid wages, and mass poverty. Coming up were actual democratic elections, a symbol of the country's new life—elections that by all forecasts Yeltsin and the democrats would lose.[35]

The Communists did not hide their plans for the economy. It was clear where they would lead. The government policy of reducing state expenditures and lowering inflation levels contradicted the view of the CPSU leadership. They believed that the budget deficit could be increased, and that the increase could be covered by printing more money. But as soon as the printing press geared up,

35 The Polish experience also suggested this. Lech Walesa, who was unquestionably a charismatic politician but who did not take responsibility for the most difficult part of the reforms, did not win the election in 1994, which was held at a time of clear dynamic growth of the Polish economy.

there would be panic on the financial markets. That would require even more printing of money, and hyperinflation would be inevitable.

The Communist program called for a price freeze in that case, particularly on groceries. It was clear that food would vanish from store shelves immediately. With fixed prices, enterprises would not be able to cover their expenses and would demand subsidies. That would mean more money emissions. In that situation international financial institutions would not give Russia loans. This would mean the end of credits and delivery of food from abroad. Default on foreign sovereign obligations would be inevitable, for no postponement on payments would be provided. However, the seizure of Russian property abroad would be a real possibility. In sum, not only would the country lose the hard-won financial stabilization of 1995, but it would be thrown back to the situation of the currency crisis of 1991, which had been so difficult to escape. Mass social protests would follow, and we know from our history how Communists react to them.

There was another side to this political crossroads. In order to implement a sensible economic policy, you need at least fifty to seventy specialists of the highest qualifications who have experience in ministries and agencies in the new market conditions. The CPSU did not have any experts like this, and no one in the government (with perhaps a few exceptions) would work with the Communists. The CPSU had people experienced in working in the Soviet economy; their chief economist was a former chairman of Gosplan, Yuri Maslyukov. With personnel like this, there was no scenario in which Zyuganov as president would not destroy the Russian economy.

In Poland, the heirs of the Communists came back to power briefly, but they did not stop market reforms. However, the Russian Communists in those years did not resemble the social democrats of Poland. Polish social democrats had not organized an armed rebellion against the president, as had the Russian Communist just two years earlier. The view of those political observers who believe that the Communists, having won power, would simply lose the next election is beyond naive. The history of the CPSU clearly shows that once they get power, Communists will not give it up without a fight. The turn that did not happen at the historic crossroads—Zyuganov's victory in 1996—would have meant a catastrophe for Russia, with the most difficult historical consequences.

A large enterprise formally considered to be state property was in fact under the control of its general director, quite often a CPSU member. The director managed its funds and other assets without being subject to any oversight. It was clear who would be the candidate he would "recommend" to the tens of thousands of workers at his plant and what financial aid he could give to Zyuganov's campaign.

This political consideration had to be kept in mind when choosing what path to take at the crossroads of the mortgage auctions: take away the Communists' commanding heights and give real content to formally legalized private property, or allow Russian history to go backward?

Technologically, the construction of mortgage auctions fit into the political schedule very well. The banks gave the state loans under the mortgage of shares for a specific time period, with the due date coming after the presidential elections. Given the huge budget deficit, it was quite likely that the state would not pay back the loans. It was clear that if Yeltsin won and the loans were not paid back, the enterprises would become the property of the banks. If Zyuganov won, the loans would not be paid back either, but the enterprises were unlikely to be given to the banks. The banks were hostages to the election results. Yeltsin's victory determined whether the banks would become owners of the enterprises or not. This economic logic was the impetus for bankers to agree in January 1996 in Davos to support Yeltsin in the elections.

Thus, the combination of economic and political factors led to the decision to hold the auctions. They played a significant role in the real transition of control of the economy into private hands. That, in turn, influenced the political alignment on the eve of the elections in 1996.

Thanks to the mortgage auctions, the goal for revenues from privatization in 1995 was reached. The budget received $1 billion that year, which was very important from the point of view of fulfilling the state's obligations to the public employees.[36] Twelve auctions were held, resulting in revenues of 5.1 trillion rubles, including 1.5 trillion rubles of canceled debts from enterprises to the state (Table 5). This can be compared to the pre-auction estimates of 2–3 trillion over twenty-nine enterprises.

The mortgage auctions are still being harshly criticized today. It must be admitted that some of the criticism is justified: the auctions were not transparent, there was no impartiality, and the rights of the third party was not observed. The winners had undoubted advantages. Of course, all court cases over the mortgage auctions confirmed the legality of the share acquisitions. Also, we cannot agree that, for the sake of beating the Communists, the enterprises—the "jewels in the crown" of the Russian empire, were given away for a song. Actually, those "pearls" were in total disarray. If you take into account the political risks, the market value of those enterprises was extremely low. It was privatization that made it possible in subsequent years to turn the dilapidated enterprises into profitable businesses. Recent serious research by independent scholars has confirmed that fact.[37]

---

36 E. G. Yasin, Rossiiskaia ekonomika. Istoki i panorama rynochnykh reform (Moscow: SU-GSE, 2002), 437.

37 Daniel Treisman, "'Loans for Shares' Revisited," National Bureau of Economic Research Working Paper Series, Working Paper 15819, www.nber.org/papers/w15819, March 2001.

Table 5

Mortgage auctions held in Russia, November–December 1995

Date	Company	Share (%)	Revenue for budget (millions of dollars)	Winner
17 November	Norilsk Nickel	51	170.1	ONEKSIMbank
8 December	YUKOS	45	159	ZAO Laguna (actually MENATEP bank)
7 December	LUKOIL	5	141	LUKOIL-Imperial
7 December	Sidanko (now TNK-BP)	51	130	MFK Bank (actually a consortium of MFK and Alfa Bank)
28 December	Sibneft	51	100.3	ZAO Neftianaia finansovaia kompaniia (guarantor Stolichny Savings Bank)
28 December	Surgutneftegaz	40.12	88.9	NPF Surgutneftegaz (guarantor ONEKSIMbank)
7 December	Novolipetsk metallurgy	14.87	31	MFK Bank (actually Renaissance Capital)
11 December	Novorossiisk Shipbuilding (Novoship)	20	22.65	Novorossiisk Shipbuilding (Novoship)
28 December	AO Nafta-Moskva	15	20.01	ZAO NaftaFin (actually management of the company)
17 November	AO Mechel	15	13	TOO Rabikom
17 November	Severo-zapadnoe River Shipbuilding	25.5	6.05	MFK Bank
7 December	Murmansk Sea Shipbuilding	23.5	4.125	ZAO Strateg (actually MENATEP bank)

Source: Wikipedia, "Privatization in Russia," http://ru.wikipedia.org/wiki/Приватизация

At the start of the election campaign in January 1996, Yeltsin's popularity was around 3–6 percent, and Zyuganov was significantly ahead of him. The actual start of the presidential campaign was the Duma election in December 1995. The ruling party, Our House Is Russia, suffered a crushing defeat, coming in third with 10 percent, and the Communists took first place with 22 percent. Added to these results along party lists, the Communists also won in majority regions, which gave them control over the State Duma. Gennady Seleznev, a Communist, was elected chairman.

Boris Yeltsin began his campaign in extremely difficult circumstances. According to Alexander Oslon, director of Obshchestrvennoe mnenie (Public

Table 6

Presidential election results, 1996

First round, 16 June

Place	Candidate	Number of votes (millions)	%
1	Boris Yeltsin	26.6	35.28
2	Gennady Zyuganov	24.2	32.03
3	Alexander Lebed	10.7	14.52
4	Grigory Yavlinsky	5.6	7.34
5	Vladimir Zhirinovsky	4.3	5.70

Second round, 3 July

1	Boris Yeltsin	40.4	53.82
2	Gennady Zyuganov	30.1	40.31
3	Against All	3.6	4.82
4			
5	Incomplete ballots		1.05

Opinion) and one of the most competent sociologists in Russia, Yeltsin's "defeat seemed inevitable" in February, when he announced his candidacy.[38] But with the help of professionals, the Yeltsin staff found unusual solutions and organized an effective election campaign. The bankers' media and financial resources played a significant part.

Yeltsin was supported in the first round primarily by Moscow and St. Petersburg, large industrial cities in northern Russia, Siberia, the Far East, a few national republics, and Russians living abroad. Zyuganov was supported primarily by residents of depressed rural regions of central Russia, the Chernozem and Volga regions, and a few republics of the northern Caucasus. It was fundamentally important that Yeltsin get first place in the first round, even if it was by only a tiny advantage, slightly over 3 percent (Table 6).

After the second round the essence of the historic crossroads became absolutely clear. We managed to get not only Yeltsin's proponents but also everyone against a return to the Communist past to unite around him. The proponents of the Communists and the most implacable opponents of the government united around Zyuganov. The results of the second round gave President Yeltsin a victory, and he was reelected for a second term.

38 Wikipedia, "Presidential Elections in Russia, 1996."

1996–2000

During the elections of 1996, as described earlier, the government formed a tactical alliance with oligarchs in order to keep the Communists from power. With the support of the nascent class of property owners and a great part of the intelligentsia, the reformers won.

However, the tactical character of this alliance was revealed right after the elections in the next strategic crossroads: who should run the state—legally elected agencies of state power, or the wealthiest businessmen in the country?

Oligarchs such as Boris Berezovsky and Vladimir Gusinsky genuinely believed that they ran the country and that they had "hired" Yeltsin to work for them as president. Their position was basically that big business should manage politicians, appoint and fire ministers, and determine which party will be allowed to have power and what policies will be implemented. Big business openly demanded the privatization of power.

The other path presumed the establishment of institutions of democracy, in which the election of the president, governors, Duma deputies, and regional legislators depended not on the oligarchs but on the citizenry. In a democracy all citizens should be equal under the law, have equal rights, and have only one way to influence policy—by uniting in a party and persuading their fellow citizens.

The choice at this crossroads was chronologically tied to the auction of the Svyazinvest company, over which the regime and business came into direct conflict. The argument was simple: would the company go to the highest bidder at an honest auction, or to its owner "by the unspoken rules"? The position of the reform wing of the government (primarily Anatoly Chubais, Boris Nemtsov, and Oleg Sysuev) was unilateral: the privatization of Svyazinvest had to guarantee the separation of business from government and the formation of a system in which the rules of the game are the same for everyone. The position of an influential part of the oligarchs was different: this was a change in the rules of the game that they did not accept.

The Svyazinvest auction was a model of honest, open, fair, and legal privatization. Its organizers did not know even a minute before the results came in who would win; that was the technology. The numbers were direct confirmation: the price started at $1.18 billion, a fantastic number for those days (it was more than all the revenues from privatization in any previous year), and in the course of harsh competitive bidding rose to $1.87 billion.

For the losing oligarchs, the price was higher than business. They considered their most important task to win victory over the government at any cost. A significant number of the oligarchs pooled their political, media, and financial resources to punish the organizers of the auction and take away Svyazinvest. Huge amounts of money were spent on bribes, buying off workers in security services, and a powerful PR attack intended to politically destroy the reform ministers. These events later became known as the First Bankers' War and the Battle of Svyazinvest.

The reformers suffered heavy damages, and some of them lost their jobs. However, Svyazinvest was not given to Berezovsky and Gusinsky, and the revenue from the sale of its shares went to primary state needs. This proved that our government could guarantee equal conditions for opposing business groups, not be the agent of any one group, and stand above when necessary. The clash of the government and oligarchs in 1997 remains one of the first successful attempts at changing the character of Russian capitalism by separating government from property.

* * *

In the meantime, the country's financial situation remained difficult. The rejection in late 1994 of emission financing of the state budget led to a sharp decrease in the growth of consumer prices (Fig. 14). However, the tightening of

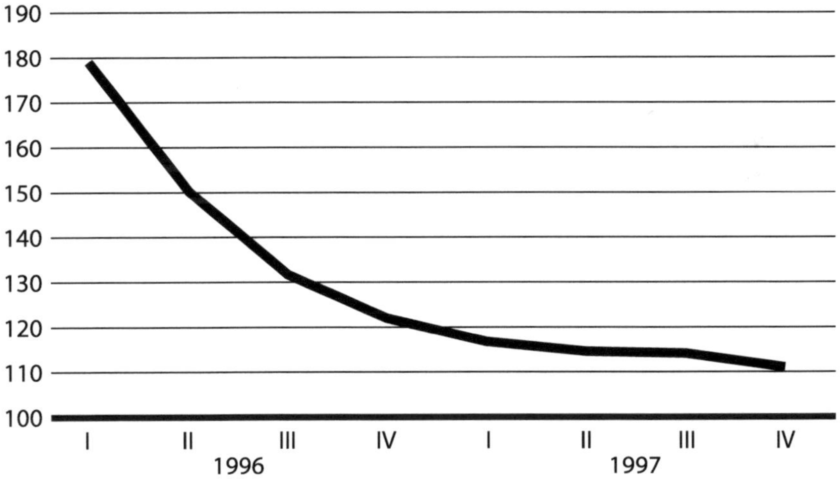

Figure 14. Growth rates of consumer prices in Russia, 1996–97 (percentage of corresponding quarter the previous year)

Source: Database SU-HSE, http://stat.hse.ru/exes/tables/CPI_Q_CHI.htm

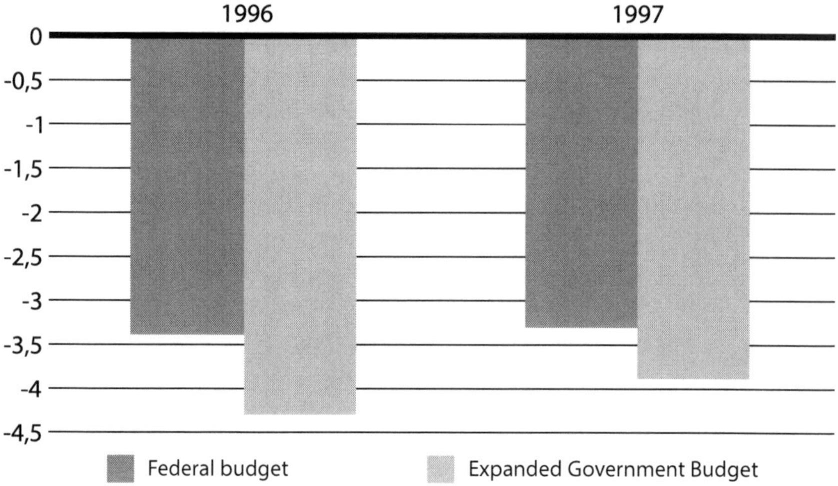

Figure 15. Deficit of the federal budget and budget of the expanded government, 1996–97 (as percentage of GDP)
Source: State Treasury, www.roskazna.ru

monetary policy under conditions of political struggle was supported only in a limited way by the tightening of budget policy (Fig. 15).

The combination of strict monetary policy (supporting a stable exchange rate for the ruble) and soft budgetary policy (covering the deficit by printing rubles) is the most important characteristic of the economic course of this period. It is well known that this combination creates risks for the stability of the financial system. However, it was necessary, for reasons rooted in the political plane. Parliament, which passes the budget, plays the key role in the formation of budgetary policy. During this period it was under the powerful influence, if not the complete control, of the Communists. The main vector of all the budget battles between the government and the parliament was the desire of the latter to raise expenditures by an unsupported hike in revenues or by an increase of the deficit from any source.

Politically, this vector was unbeatable: at the budget formation stage the Communists looked like the defenders of village workers, civil servants (which includes teachers and doctors), and the military-industrial complex, and at the implementation stage (or, rather, the inevitable lack of implementation), they appeared as harsh critics of the failures of the government, which was unable to deliver on its promises. This is precisely why the government and the Central Bank had to compensate for the weak budgetary policy with an even stricter monetary policy. This kind of contradictory policy, when the budget is unbalanced and the Ministry of Finance needs the Central Bank to cover budget expenses, cannot be maintained for long. Sooner or later trust in the stability of

Table 7

Domestic state debt of Russia, the United States, Japan, and Germany, 1996–97 (end of year, percentage of GDP)

	Russia	Germany**	United States*	Japan**
1996	18.2	57.9	67.3	100.5
1997	21.0	57.1	65.6	107.2

* Federal public debt
** General government debt (gross)
Sources: Ministry of Finance of Russian Federation; U.S. Office of Management and Budget, www.whitehouse.gov/omb/budget/fy2010/assets/hist.pdf; for Japan and Germany, IMF, World Economic Outlook, April 2009

the national currency will be lost. The Russian authorities tried to resolve this contradiction by increasing state debt.

This was a risky tactic but the only one that made sense. In 1977, the Russian domestic state debt as a percentage of GDP was modest by international standards (Table 7). And the economic growth that began in 1997 gave us hope that the ratio of the debt and GDP was stabilizing.

Economic growth began later in Russia than in Eastern Europe. This is not hard to understand given the longer period of the socialist experiment in Rus-

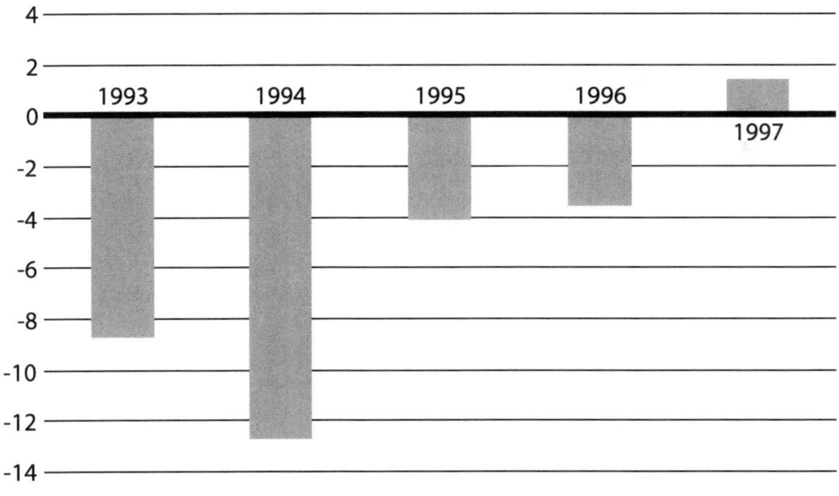

Figure 16. Rate of economic growth or decline in Russia, 1993–97 (percentage of previous year)
Source: IMF, World Economic Outlook, April 2009

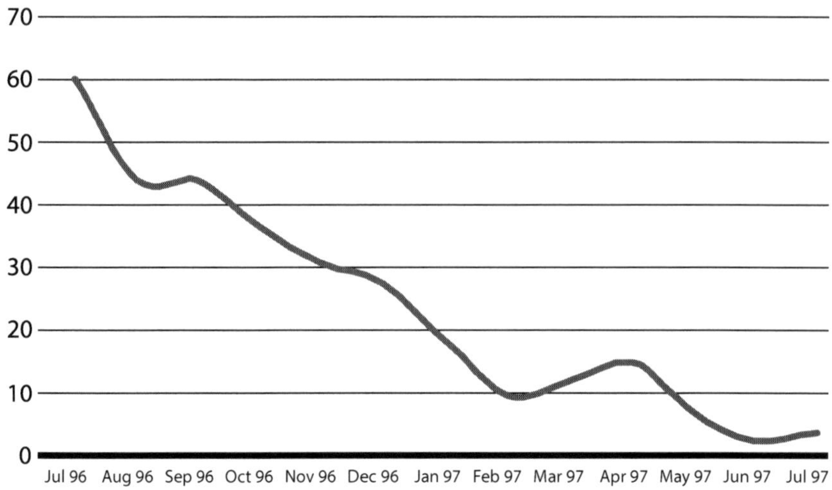

Figure 17. Real GKO interest rate, July 1996–July 1997 (percent)

Note: The real GKO interest rate is calculated on the basis of inflation over the preceding six months, expressed annually, and equals the average income on GKOs on the secondary market for all terms minus changes on the consumer price index for the preceding six months, expressed annually. From September 1995 through March 1996, the average income on GKOs is based on the above for the preceding three months.

Source: Obzor ekonomiki Rossii. Osnovnye tendentsii razvitiia, II kvartal 1996-IV kvartal 1997 godov// Rossisko-evropejskii tsentr ekonomicheskoj politiki (Moscow: 1997, 1998), www.budgetrf.ru/Publications/Magazines/recep/RECP_index0.htm

sia and the structural disproportions related to the militarization of the Soviet economy. But in 1997, economic growth became a reality (Figure 16). Hence the enthusiasm of investors prepared to invest money in Russia.

In 1997, the interest rates on state short-term bonds (GKO) went down (Fig. 17). In real terms they were close to zero. However, Russia's credit rating gradually stabilized beginning in 1996 (Table 8).[39]

However, the combination of soft budgetary policy and strict monetary policy, the openness of the economy, the growing dependence of domestic finance on the ebb and flow of capital to the developing markets, the dependence of the country's balance of payment on the production of raw materials, which is hard to predict and can vary significantly, created risks for the steadiness of economic growth and financial stability.

Thus, by the end of 1997, the economy, which continued to be vulnerable to external factors, had nevertheless entered the zone of economic growth for the

39 Editor's note: This fact was highly rated by experts. In 1997, Euromoney magazine recognized Anatoly Chubais as the best finance minister of the year: www.euromoney.com:80/Article/1005909/Finance-Minister-of-the-Year-Chubais-forces-the-pace.html?p=2.

Table 8

Russia's credit rating according to Standard & Poor's, 1996–99

Date	Rating on international scale		Rating on national scale
	In foreign currency/outlook	In national currency/outlook	
7 Oct 1996	BB-/Stable/B	—/—/—	—
19 Dec 1997	BB-/Negative/B	—/—/—	—
27 May 1998	BB/CreditWatch Negative/B	—/—/—	—
9 Jun 1998	B+/Stable/B	—/—/—	—
13 Aug 1998	B-/Negative/C	—/—/—	—
17 Aug 1998	CCC/Negative/C	—/—/—	—
16 Sep 1998	CCC-/Negative/C	—/—/—	—
27 Jan 1999	SD —/SD	—/—/—	—
7 May 1999	SD/—/SD	CCC/Stable/C	—

Source: Standard & Poor's

first time since the 1980s. The combination of all domestic economic and political factors gave Russia a real chance to turn the nascent economic growth into a long-term growth. But problems came from an unexpected source.

By the mid-1990s, Southeast Asia was considered a model of economic growth. The expressions "Southeast Asian economic miracle" and "Asian tigers" were commonplace in newspaper headlines. Many expert works are devoted to the causes of such dynamic growth and financial stability over so many years.[40] Some authors discussed the problem of steadiness of the economic growth in this region, but there was no concrete analysis of the possibility of a crisis there.[41]

The world economy has changed over the last two hundred years. The configuration of financial and monetary systems that existed at the moment of the

40 Kihwan Kim, "The 1997–1998 Korean Financial Crisis: Causes, Policy Response, and Lessons," 2006, www.imf.org/external/np/seminars/eng/2006/cpem/pdf/kihwan.pdf; N. Crafts, "East Asian Growth Before and After the Crisis," IMF Working Paper 98/137, September 1998; K. Kochhar, P. Loungani, and M. R. Stone, "The East Asian Crisis: Macroeconomic Developments and Policy Lessons," IMF Working Paper 99/28, August 1998; A. Berg, "The Asia Crisis: Causes, Policy Responses, and Outcomes," IMF Working Paper 98/138, October 1999; T. J. T. Balino and A. Ubide, "The Korean Financial Crisis of 1997 — A Strategy Financial Sector Reform," IMF Working Paper 99/28, March 1999; Jong-Wha Lee and E. Borensztein, "Financial Crisis and Credit Crunch in Korea: Evidence from Firm Level Data," IMF Working Paper 00/25, February 2000.

41 P. Krugman, "The Myth of Asia's Miracle," Foreign Affairs 73, no. 6 (November–December 1994): 62–78.

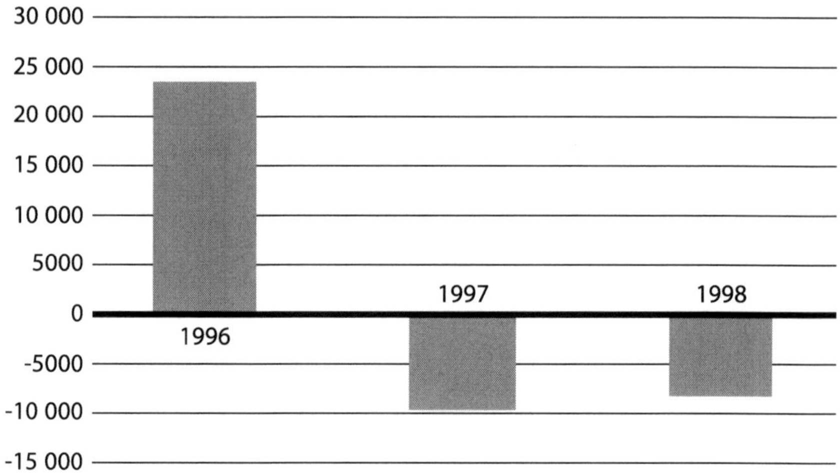

Figure 18. Balance of inflow or outflow of capital* in South Korea, 1996–98 (millions of dollars)

* Balance of the account of capital operations and the financial account

Source: IMF, International Financial Statistics database (CD-ROM), June 2009

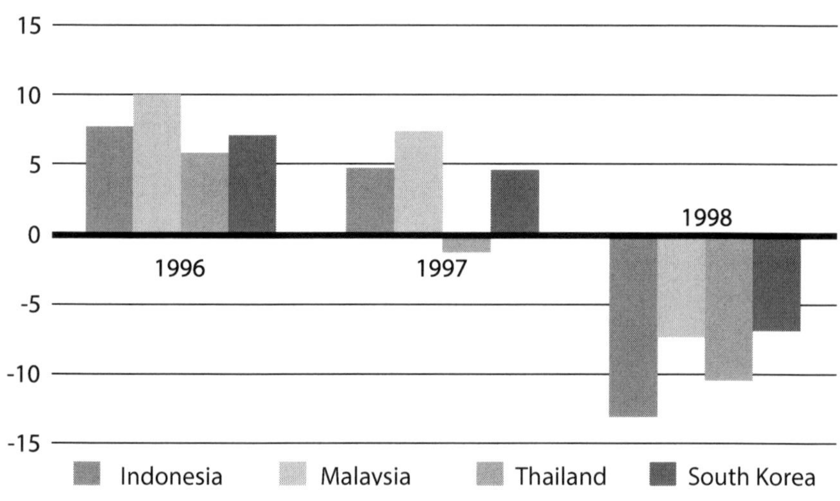

Figure 19. Growth of GDP in Indonesia, Malaysia, Thailand, and South Korea, 1996–98 (percentage of previous year)

Source: World Bank, World Development Indicators, 2009

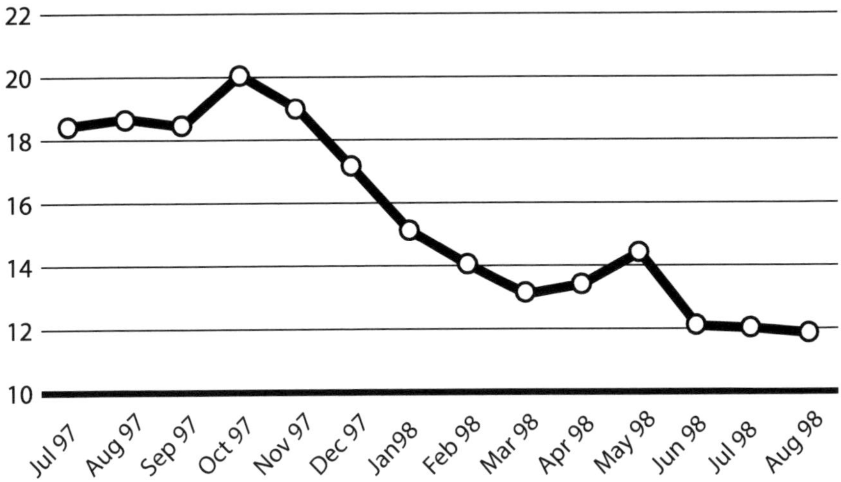

Figure 20. Brent oil price dynamics, July 1997–August 1998 (dollars per barrel)
Source: IMF

crisis in Southeast Asia (the absence of a gold currency standard, floating exchange rates of world reserve currencies, open capital markets) had formed comparatively recently, in the 1970s and 1980s. The expert community did not understand how this system worked, so there were no specialists able to foresee either the Mexican crisis of 1994 or the crisis in Southeast Asia in 1997–98.[42]

An important factor that affected the dynamic of economic growth was the sharp and unexpected (for most experts and investors) change in the balance between income and outgo of capital in the countries of Southeast Asia (Fig. 18). It was followed by radical changes in growth rates in these economies (Fig. 19).

Investors feared that the events in some developing countries could spread to other economies with comparable levels of development, such as those in Latin America and the post-Soviet space, and they began removing financial resources from such markets. In these situations investors' main concerns are related not to the long-term prospects of the economy but to the protection of the funds they have invested. The time horizon for key decisions is short. For countries belonging to developing markets and having a lot of short-term loans, this creates major problems. This holds in particular for countries where the financial and payments balance depends on the prices of raw materials (Fig. 20).

42 R. M. Entov, "Nekotorye problemy issledovaniia delovikh tsiklov," Finansovyi krizis v Rossii i v mire, ed. Ye. T. Gaidar (Moscow: Prospekt, 2009): 6–39.

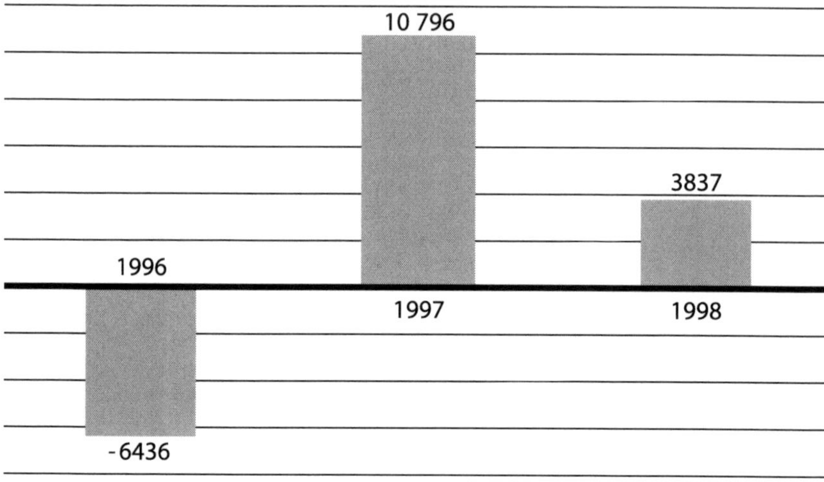

Figure 21. Inflow or outflow of capital* in Russia, 1996–98 (millions of dollars)
* Balance of account of operations with capital and financial instruments
Source: IMF

It is not hard for investors to understand that the raw materials markets affect financial markets. Hence their natural reaction, which is to move money away from riskier markets (Fig. 21).

The positive trends that started in the Russian economy made it possible, in part, to establish and build up gold currency reserves. In July 1997 those reserves had reached 10.3 percent of GDP ($24.4 billion) in Russia; in Brazil the comparable figure was only 7 percent of GDP ($63.8 billion).[43] Nevertheless, the developing crisis in Southeast Asia put both countries into a zone of high economic risk.

Thus the nascent Russian market economy took two blows—the sharp decline in oil prices, and the crisis that started in Southeast Asia and spread to Latin America. The crisis affected more than twenty states. In Thailand, South Korea, Philippines, Argentina, and Estonia, it led to a change of government. In Indonesia and the Philippines, the constitutional electoral process was violated. Indonesia in 1998 and Argentina in 2001 saw bloody clashes between demonstrators and the regime, with injuries and fatalities (Table 9).

In the changed financial and economic situation, with falling prices for the export goods that made up the basis of the balance of payments, an important crossroads appeared: radically lower the exchange rate of the national currency, or preserve its relative stability?

43 Central Bank, Russian Federation, www.cbr.ru; IMF, International Financial Statistics (CD-ROM), April 2009.

Table 9

The world economic crisis of 1997–99

Events	Countries
Experienced significant economic crises	Indonesia, Thailand, Malaysia, South Korea, Hong Kong, Japan, Singapore, Philippines, Russia, Kazakhstan, Lithuania, Estonia, Moldova, Brazil, Argentina, Chile, Colombia, Bolivia, Uruguay, Ecuador, Paraguay, Venezuela
Of them, the opposition came to power through elections during the period or as a result of the crisis	Thailand (1997), South Korea (1997), Philippines (1998), Argentina (1999), Estonia (1999)
Of them, the opposition came to power through special elections	Thailand (1997)
The opposition came to power without elections (the normal electoral process was violated)	Indonesia (1998), Philippines (2001)
Bloody mass clashes with the authorities, with fatalities	Indonesia (1998), Argentina (2001)

Source: Materials presented by S. Zhavoronkov and S. Shulgin, Institute of the Economy in Transition

Either decision was risky. A radical reduction in the exchange rate was a threat to the stability of the banking system. With the combination of strict monetary policy and soft budgetary policy, the banking system guarantees contracts on hard currency loans. But with a large-scale devaluation of the national currency, repaying loans is difficult. The decision to lower the exchange rate means, in essence, the bankruptcy of the largest private banks, entailing bank panics, loss of deposits, paralysis of the system of loans to the real sector, and the end of economic growth. Public opinion, especially in the political space, would hold the government and the Central Bank to blame for this catastrophic situation, for having taken steps toward devaluation.

Rejecting devaluation of the ruble was also risky, as it raised the real possibility of loss of the country's currency reserves. A high demand for currency at a beneficial rate for buyers, which the Central Bank would have to support, would quickly deplete its currency reserves. The Brazilian monetary and financial authorities recognized this challenge before the Russians did. They made corrections in their monetary and budgetary policies almost as soon as the Southeast Asian crisis began.

At the time, the Russian authorities were paralyzed by the conflict between the young reformer government and the oligarchs, and unlike the Brazilians, they reacted later. The consequences were heavy: investors lost confidence in Russia's ability to meet its financial obligations.

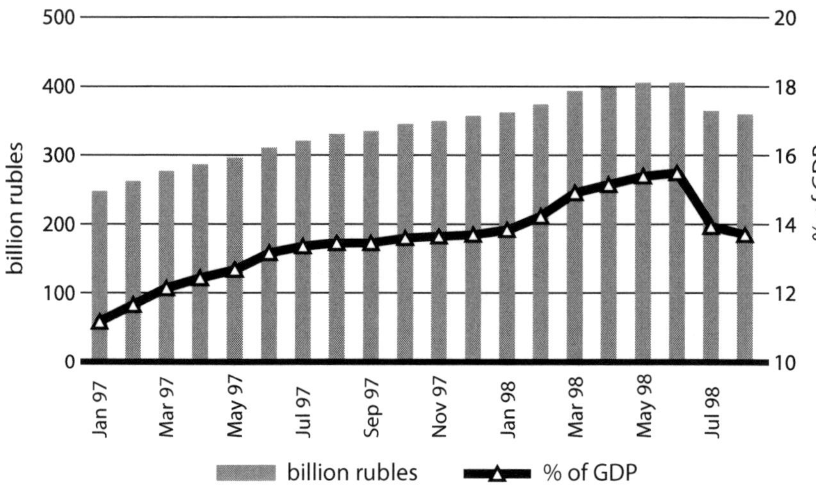

Figure 22. Dynamics of the state debt on GKO-OFZ, January 1997–August 1998

In April 1998, the president decided to propose Sergei Kiriyenko as chairman of the government. The new government understood very well that to protect the economy from the looming external crisis, they needed a program of tough measures, and in this they were supported by international financial institutions. Such a program was quickly elaborated. In June, the president appointed his representative for negotiations. Without going into detail, we will note the most important point: in the complex negotiations that place in the summer of 1998, we managed to coordinate with the IMF and World Bank a package of measures for financial stabilization and the needed resources in the amount of $25 billion. However, the Communist-controlled State Duma refused to pass it.[44] From the political point of view, the deputies were in a win-win situation: fighting against what they portrayed as the "enslavement of Russia by international capital through foreign loans," they got support for actions that inevitably led to economic catastrophe, creating a terrible blow against the president and government and opening up a path to power for themselves.

Investors quickly understood what had happened, and by early August 1998 they came to the conclusion: get money out of Russia fast.

By 14–15 August 1998 it was clear: if the tendencies of the financial market did not change, the gold currency reserves would be depleted and Russia would

44 Sergei Kiriyenko noted that originally the package of stabilization legislation expected revenues of 102.2 billion rubles. However, the government laws passed by the Duma, according to the premier, could bring in only 37.8 billion rubles. In order to balance and compensate for the losses from the anticrisis laws the parliament refused to pass, the government had to act through presidential decrees and cabinet resolutions. Izvestia, 22 July 1998.

again find itself in the situation that the USSR had faced in November 1991 (and which Russia had avoided in January 1995).

A new crossroads arose: give up trying to stop inflation and go back to printing money to finance the state budget and to pay off the GKO debt, or go directly to default on government bonds?

For all the drama of these alternatives, they had to be examined extremely rationally in a very short and emotional time.

The state's debts on GKO-OFZ as of 1 August 1998 were 363 billion rubles, which was roughly equal to the planned revenues of the federal budget (Fig. 22). In August 1998 the government was borrowing around 15 billion rubles weekly, of which 8 billion went to pay bonds issued earlier, leaving 7 billion rubles for health care, education, social welfare, defense spending, and maintenance of state services.

According to the calculations made at the Institute for the Economy in Transition, using emission to finance GKO-OFZ debt would have increased the amount of money in circulation between August and December 1998 by approximately 150 percent, which would bring inflation to levels of 10–12 percent a month. In other words, consumer prices would rise 45–50 percent in 1998 and 120–140 percent in 1999.

There was no certainty that agricultural producers would be willing to deliver goods to the cities at that inflation level. World economic history did not fill us with optimism that this problem was solvable.

We chose the second alternative, which also was extremely unpleasant, and which was related to the consequences (described above) of the forced soft budgetary policy of 1995–97: default on state securities. It was clear that this decision would be a blow to the attractiveness of investment in the Russian economy, to the stability of the banking system, and to the preservation of people's savings. In many ways it repeated the experience of South Korea, which took similar actions in December 1997; there the moves were adequate.[45] Our choice was supported by world financial institutions, including the IMF. The decision to default on GKOs and devalue the ruble was made between 14 and 16 August and announced on 17 August 1998. More than 90 percent of holders of state bonds in Russia agreed to the restructuring conditions proposed by the authorities.[46]

---

45 Kihwan Kim, "The 1997–1998 Korean Financial Crisis: Causes, Policy Response, and Lessons," 2006, www.imf.org/external/np/seminars/eng/2006/cpem/pdf/kihwan.pdf; T. J.T. Balino and A. Ubide, "The Korean Financial Crisis of 1997—A Strategy Financial Sector Reform," IMF Working Paper 99/28, March 1999; Jong-Wha Lee and E. Borensztein, "Financial Crisis and Credit Crunch in Korea: Evidence from Firm Level Data," IMF Working Paper 00/25, February 2000.

46 B. Zlatkis, "Depozitarium," Rynok tsennykh bumag supplement, 2006, no. 11: 33–34.

Table 10

Losses from the 1998 crisis

Losses	Percentage of GDP
Total losses in Russian economy	3.5
Including:	
Reduction in national saving due to loss of capital in banking system	2.5
Devaluation of investments by individuals and enterprises due to bank insolvency and delays in payments in conditions of inflation	0.7
Losses by enterprises caused by accounts crisis	0.2
Losses by budget system as a result of inflationary devaluation of tax payments, stuck in insolvent banks	0.1

Note: Some of the losses of the Russian banking system were the reverse side of the budget's win, because it had shifted the responsibility for solving the problems of the budgetary and debt crisis onto banks and the public and sharply reduced expenditures on servicing the state debt thanks to the freeze and restructuring of GKO-OFZ and the default on bonds issued within the framework of restructuring the Soviet debt to the London Club.
Source: www.vedi.ru/o_cr/cr0015_r.htm, 1999

Table 11

Consequences of the 1998 crisis

The solvency of banks decreased sharply and the number of bankruptcies grew. While in the first quarter of 1998 problem banks constituted around 30 percent of all banks, by 1 October it was almost 50 percent, and some 40–45 percent of bank assets were concentrated in them. The number of commercial banks went down 13 percent in 1998 (from 1,697 to 1,476).
Bank assets went down as the result of devaluation of securities and an increase in the share of dubious and hopeless debts in the banks' credit portfolios. The working assets of banks went down from 20 percent of GDP in January 1998 to 15 percent in January 1999, and, without the effect of overvaluation of hard currency credits, to 9.6 percent of GDP.
The public and enterprises took out a significant portion of their savings from the banking system.
The economy was struck by a massive accounts crisis, in which both the enterprises and the budget system suffered significant losses.
The losses of the banking system were estimated at 50–60 percent of the banking capital, and direct losses reached 25–30 percent.

Source: www.vedi.ru/o_cr/cr0015_r.htm

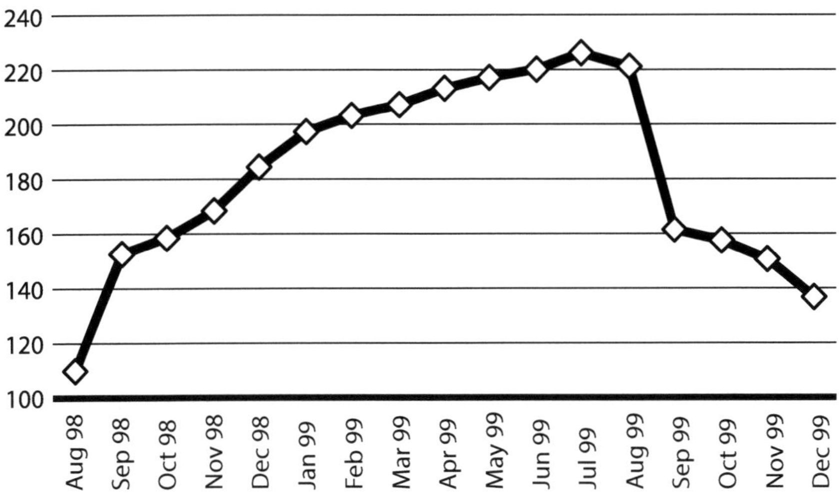

Figure 23. Index of consumer prices, August 1998–December 1999 (percentage of corresponding period the previous year)
Source: Database, SU-HSE, http://stat.hse.ru/exes/tables/CPI_M_CHI.htm

* * *

The crisis and default of August 1998 led to immediate severe consequences for the population and the country's entire economy (Tables 10 and 11).

For the first time in many years there was a mood of panic over the shortages of mass consumer goods.[47] The threats of hyperinflation and paralysis in the delivery of food to cities, which had receded into the past during the early 1990s, were once again topics of discussion (Fig. 23).

It was particularly painful that the nascent middle class suffered most from the crisis. These were the people who believed in the new economy and had started their own businesses. Hundreds of thousands of barely acclimated private owners lost their businesses, and millions of people lost jobs.

The political price for the August 1998 default was extremely high. Support for President Yeltsin, who had announced just days before the default that the

47 "All Goods Will Be More Expensive," Kommersant, 18 August 1998; A. Kaledina, "Stores Don't Care About Boris Fedorov," Kommersant, 19 August 1998; A. Kaledina, "Demand for Goods Is Rising with the Prices," Kommersant, 26 August 1998; A. Kaledina, "Nothing Left for Pensioners but Bread," Kommersant, 27 August 1998, 157; A. Kaledina, "Back to the Future," 28 August 1998; A. Kaledina, "And Once Again," Kommersant, 29 August 1998; A. Kaledina, "There Is Enough Food for Now," Kommersant, 1 September 1998; V. Esipov and A. Smirnov, "St. Petersburg May Be Left with No Bread," Kommersant, 4 September 1998; A. Kaledina, "Shortages," Kommersant, 5 September 1998.

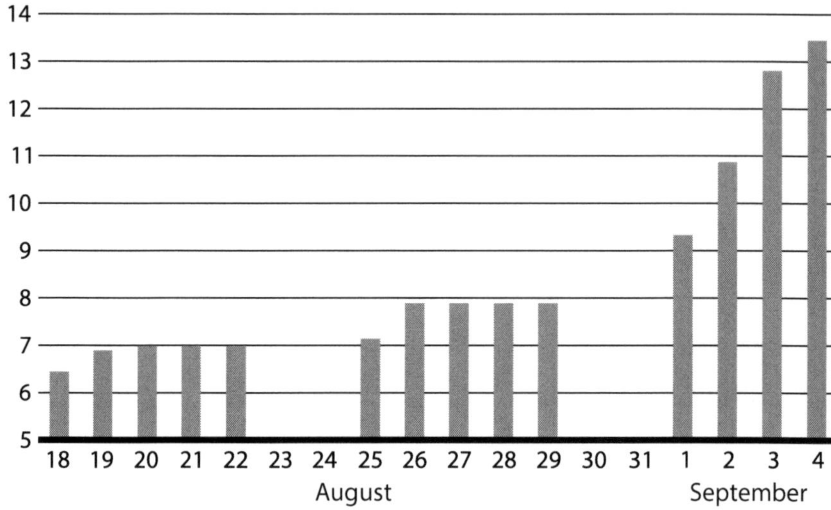

Figure 24. Exchange of ruble to dollar, 17 August–4 September 1998 (rubles per dollar)
Source: Central Bank, Russian Federation

ruble would not be devalued,[48] was undermined, and the government of "young reformers" headed by Kiriyenko was fired, as was the leadership of the Central Bank. These were the people who had negotiated the terms and the program of financial stabilization with the IMF and agreed upon financial aid. Now that they were no longer in their posts, this effectively relieved the leadership of the International Monetary Fund of the obligations they had committed to. Returned to the White House for a short time as acting prime minister, Victor Chernomyrdin announced before the discussion in the Duma of his candidacy that there was a need for controlled emissions and a return to financing the budget deficit by credits from the Central Bank. The ruble plummeted against the dollar (Fig. 24).

In this situation President Yeltsin engaged in a unique and extremely risky political maneuver: appointing the first leftist government in the history of reform Russia, headed by Yevgeny Primakov. For all the new premier's personal loyalty to the president (in the previous five years Yeltsin had appointed him to the post of head of the Foreign Intelligence Service and then to be minister of foreign affairs), key posts in the government were assigned to moderate leftists who had support from the Communist majority in the State Duma.

The country yet again faced a historic crossroads: return to socialism, or continue building a market economy based on private property?

48 N. Timakova and S. Brutman, "Everything Is Going Fine—The President Is Resting N.," Kommersant, 15 August 1998.

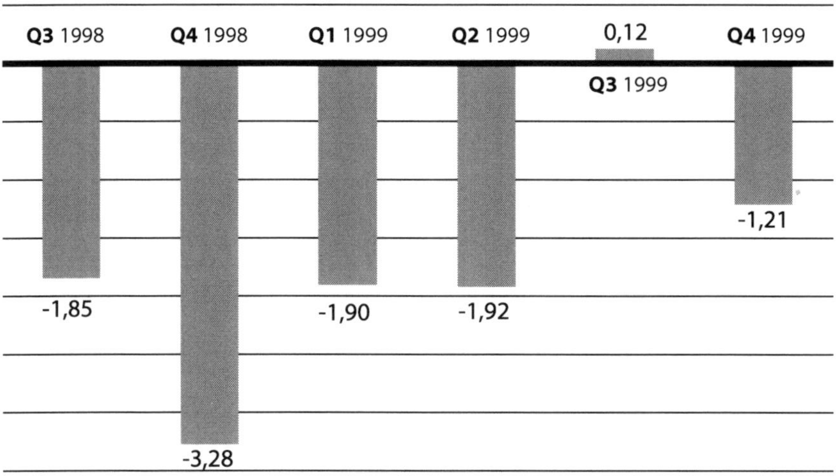

Figure 25. Deficit or surplus of the Russian Federation consolidated budget, Q3 1998–Q4 1999 (percentage of GDP)
Source: Roskazna

The mass media were filled with assertions that the crisis had put an end to Russian reforms, proving their unsustainability; that market transformations were impossible in Russia; and that a third path must be found. There were forecasts of coming nationalization, the resurrection of Gosplan, and unlimited monetary emission.

The government faced a choice: do what the parliamentary majority had been proposing for many years—that is, reject the support of the IMF and World Bank and return to emission financing of the budget, which would mean hyperinflation and its predictable consequences—or return to a conservative fiscal policy and accept the inflationary surge in late August and September 1998, as it would lower the state's financial obligations and create a base for the subsequent reduction of inflation.

The personal factor played a significant role here as well. Primakov, a highly experienced politician, understood that if he accepted the advice of the left-wingers, this time those political forces and he personally would be held responsible.

The Primakov government did not accept the suggestion to return private property back to the state, establish price controls, and increase issuance of currency. Passing a minimum of regulations, it maintained political stability despite the sharp drop in standard of living and the banking crisis. After nine months with Yevgeny Primakov in power, the country had a budget surplus, an agreement with the IMF and World Bank on credits, and the same economic policy as the previous government (Fig. 25).

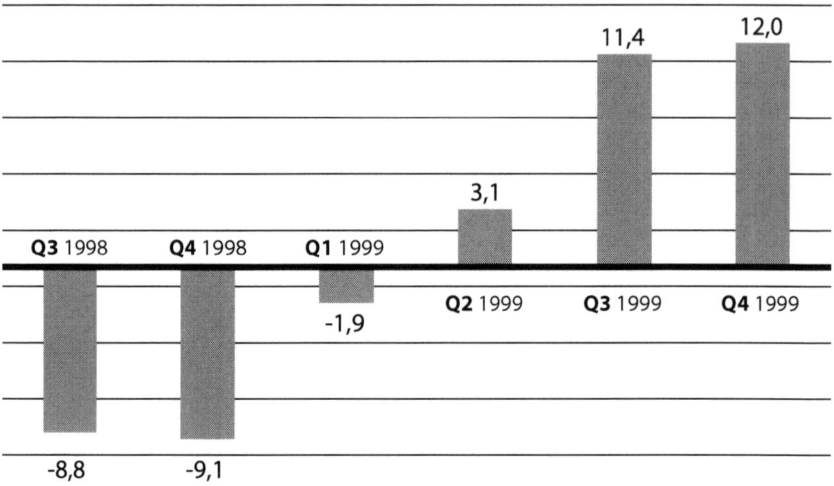

Figure 26. Rate of increase of GDP, Q3 1998–Q4 1999 (percentage of corresponding period the previous year)

Source: Database, SU-HSE, http://stat.hse.ru/exes/tables/GDP_Q_I.htm

The experiment in fall 1998 showed that a leftist government was unable to turn the country backward toward the "radiant Soviet past." It also demonstrated that the way out of the crisis and toward further development of the economy required macroeconomic stabilization based on private property.

The left-wingers who came to power in 1998 found that they were unable to carry out a single one of their promises—nationalization of industry, abolition of the circulation of dollars, or introduction of state controls on prices. This historical experiment showed that the market transformations set the framework for making global economic decisions. The leftists could not break out of that framework.

The mechanisms of the market economy had matured to the extent that their reaction to the crisis was adequate. The inefficient and unprofitable enterprises went bust, while the companies that were capable of growth and development prospered. The long-range consequences of the default and the Primakov government's subsequent actions meant that Russia's economic growth, which had begun in 1997 and been interrupted by the crisis of 1997–98, revived in early 1999 and remained steady through the following decade (Fig. 26).

The country's finances stabilized (Fig. 27).

In the spring of 1999, the Communists, inspired by the positive economic climate, used their parliamentary majority to attack Boris Yeltsin and call for a vote on impeaching the president.[49] Yeltsin's response was typical of his political style: he fired the Primakov government. The impeachment vote was

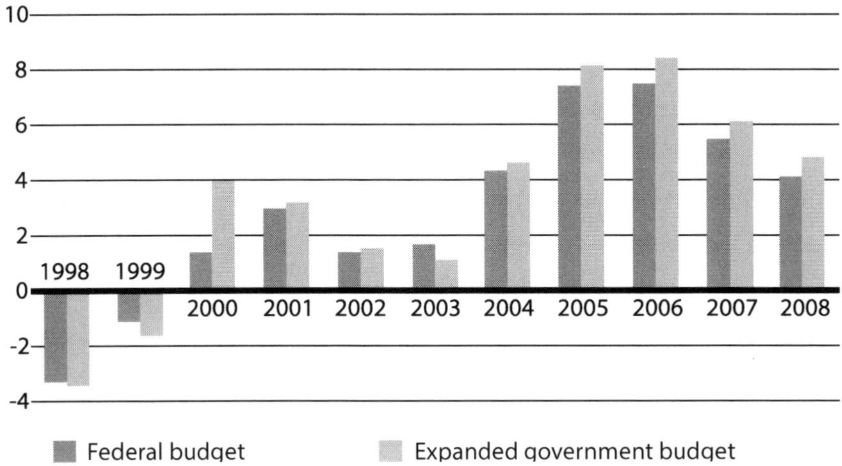

Figure 27. Balance* of the federal budget and the budget of the expanded government, 1998–2000 (percentage of GDP)

* Minus is deficit, plus is surplus

Source: Roskazna

unsuccessful, as the Communists' simple majority was not sufficient for a constitutional majority on such questions. They could not get the necessary 300 votes on any of the charges: 239 deputies voted for the charge of breaking up the USSR, 263 for the charge on the events of 1993, 241 for the charge on ruining the army, 283 for the charge on the war in Chechnya, and 238 for the charge of genocide of the Russian people. And then Yeltsin brought to a brilliant finish his unique political experiment: having appointed the first left-wing government in the history of post-Soviet Russia, he now fired it.

49 D. Kamyshev, "Face of Impeachment," Kommersant, 14 May 1999; "The Duma Will Be on the President's Leash," Kommersant, 14 May 1999; D. Kamyshev, "Epidemic in the Duma," Kommersant, 15 May 1999; "Report from the State Duma," Zavtra, 18 May 1999.

2000–2008

The next crossroads that was widely discussed in the press was not a real one, in our opinion. It boiled down to the question of whether Yeltsin would consider it possible and necessary to stay for a third term. We were certain that it was impossible. It contradicted the Constitution, which he had approved, and it contradicted the ideas of the first president of Russia on the rights and freedoms of Russian citizens.

After the removal of the Primakov government, Yeltsin was free to select a candidate for president. Why he chose Vladimir Putin is a question only Yeltsin could answer. However, it is a statistically proven fact that economic growth in Russia, which had begun in 1997 and faltered during the subsequent crisis, revived beginning in mid-1999 under prime ministers Yevgeny Primakov and then Sergei Stepashin.

The crossroads that faced the new president was extremely simple: implement the economic reforms that had been elaborated during Yeltsin's second term but not realized because of the lack of support from the Duma, or reject them?

A reminder of the background for this decision: in 1999, economic growth was only just becoming reestablished after the crisis of 1998 (Fig. 28). Today it

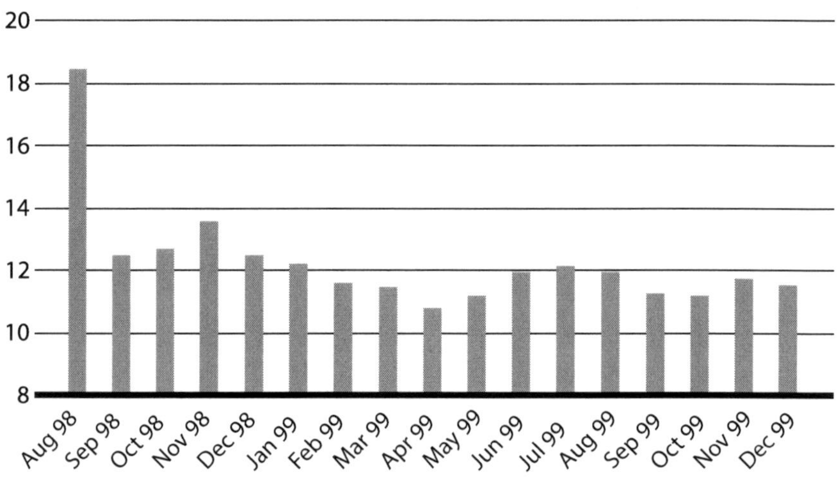

Figure 28. Gold currency reserves of the Russian Federation, August 1998–December 1999 (billions of dollars)

Source: Central Bank, Russian Federation

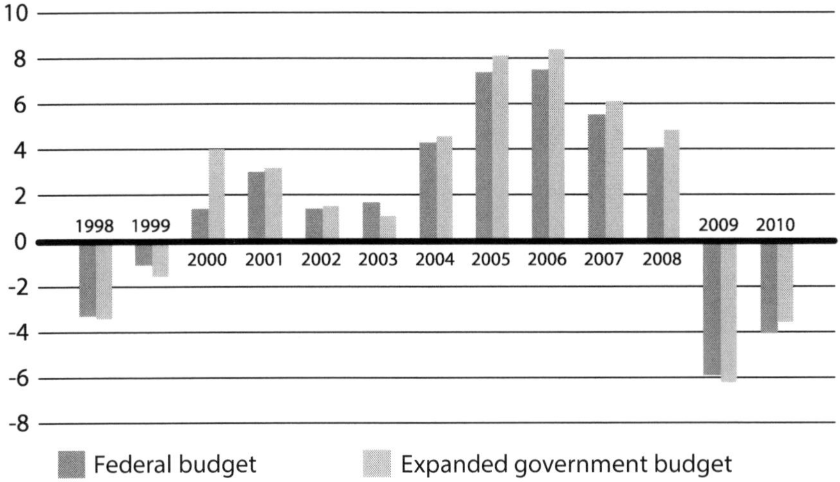

Figure 29. Balance of the federal budget and the expanded government budget of the Russian Federation, 1998–2010 (percentage of GDP) [minus is deficit, plus is surplus]
Source: Roskazna

seems obvious that the steady economic growth that began in 1999 would last. At the time, however, few people believed it.[50]

After the default of 1998, access to hard currency credits was limited. The obligations for servicing foreign debt, which would have to be paid in the next few years, were high. In these conditions, it was dangerous for the political elite that had come to power at the end of 1999 and early in 2000 to reject reforms that could lay the foundation for financial stability and steady economic growth. Instead, the new government chose a different option: using the parliamentary majority to implement economic reforms. The advantage was that the contours of these reforms had already been sketched during Yeltsin's second term.

These plans encompassed tax reform, including the introduction of a flat income tax and a reduction of the tax on profit, with a limit on subsidies; reform of taxation of income from natural rents, and the regulation of export duties on natural resources; and reform of fiscal federalism. All revenues from the VAT were sent to the federal budget, and income tax revenues went to regional budgets. Oth-

50 The government and the Central Bank consider the pessimistic outlook on growth of GDP, money mass, and income most likely. (D. Cherkasov, A. Nikolsky. "A Purely Mathematical Killing," Izvestiya, 6 October 1999); "The calculations of independent experts and specialists of the Ministry of the Economy show that in these conditions we can expect growth of 7-8 percent for 1999 and no more than 1.5 percent the following year. The transition to a negative dynamic can be expected by the middle of next year." (N. Kirichenko. "The Budget of the Transitional Period," Izvestiya, 13 October 1999).

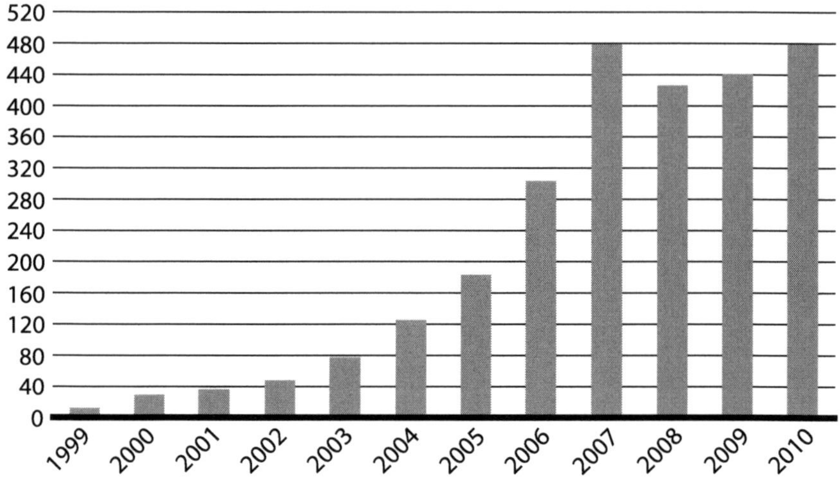

Figure 30. Gold currency reserves of Russia, 1999–2010 (end of year; billions of dollars)
Source: Central Bank, Russian Federation

er elements of the reform were the creation of rights for private sale of land and the creation of the Stabilization Fund, which would temper the effects of fluctuations in raw materials prices on the country's balance of payments and budget system.

This along with the transformations of the 1990s laid the foundation of the Russian economy's dynamic growth between 2000 and 2008 and of the country's financial stability (Figs. 29 and 30).

By 2003 it was clear that the crisis processes related to the collapse of the Soviet economy were behind us, the economy was growing dynamically, and it financial position was steady (Table 12).

In these circumstances, the Russian authorities saw an expansion of their freedom to maneuver in economic, domestic, and foreign policy. The "problem of 2003," about which so much had been said in early 2000, stayed in the past.[51]

---

51 "The '2003 problem' consists of three basic factors—foreign debt, wear and tear of production means, and demographic decline. Russia had to pay its debts of $17 billion in 2003. Also a significant deterioration of production facilities was expected in 2003. This means infrastructure. The third main threat was demographic decline, related to aging of the population." Cf. "Russia Is Already Battling the '2003 Problem,'" Lenta.ru, http://lenta.ru/russia/2000/09/12/bug2003. "The essence of the problem is this: the level of deterioration of means will reach critical levels by 2003, which will mean a wave of technogenic catastrophes, blips in energy and fuel networks, collapse of buildings, transportation accidents. ... It should be noted that three storms are expected to break in 2003: along with the amortization crisis we are describing in this article, there will also be a worsening of the demographic situation, forecast by specialists, plus the due date that year of payments on foreign state debts." M. Zhilkina, "Rotted Through," Russkii polis, 2002, no. 8: 46–47.

Table 12

Russia's credit rating according to Standard & Poor's, 1999–2003

Date	International scale rating		National scale rating
	Foreign currency/outlook	National currency/outlook	
3 Nov 2003	BB/Stable/B	BB+/Stable/B	—
5 Dec 2002	BB/Stable/B	BB+/Stable/B	—
26 Jul 2002	BB-/Stable/B	BB-/Stable/B	—
22 Feb 2002	B+/Positive/B	B+/Positive/B	ruAA+
19 Dec 2001	B+/Stable/B	B+/Stable/B	—
4 Oct 2001	B/Positive/B	B/Positive/B	—
28 Jun 2001	B/Stable/B	B/Stable/B	—
8 Dec 2000	B-/Stable/C	B-/Stable/C	—
27 Jul 2000	SD/—/SD	B-/Stable/C	—
15 Feb 2000	SD/—/SD	CCC+/Positive/C	—
7 May 1999	SD/—/SD	CCC/Stable/C	—
27 Jan 1999	SD/—/SD	—/—/—	—

Source: Standard & Poor's

Two issues came to the foreground: What kind of relations should be developed with big business, with the people who had been called oligarchs in the late 1990s? And what should be done with the political system?

In early 2003, the oligarchs were still influential. They controlled the Duma majority; without their support it was hard to get the laws the government wanted passed, including those that were important for the budget process. Russian oligarchs hired experts with experience lobbying the U.S. Congress. Those experts knew how to include amendments beneficial for big business in laws that could not be vetoed by the president. This is a century-old process in Washington. But Moscow is not Washington. There is no stable democracy of taxpayers here. Hence the conflict between YUKOS and the regime. YUKOS had the support of the oil lobby and serious influence in the Duma; the president had executive power and the ability to use state force to solve a problem.

The problem was simple: try to find a compromise, or have a confrontation? Both sides chose confrontation.[52]

52 Platon Lebedev was arrested 2 July 2003. D. Butrin, P. Sapozhnikov, A. Gerasimov, and D. Skorobogat'ko, "They Came for YUKOS," Kommersant, 2 July 2003. Mikhail Khodorkovsky was arrested on 25 October 2003. M. Lepina, S. Topol', V. Romanov, and K. Voronov, "Jail Time," Kommersant, 27 October 2003.

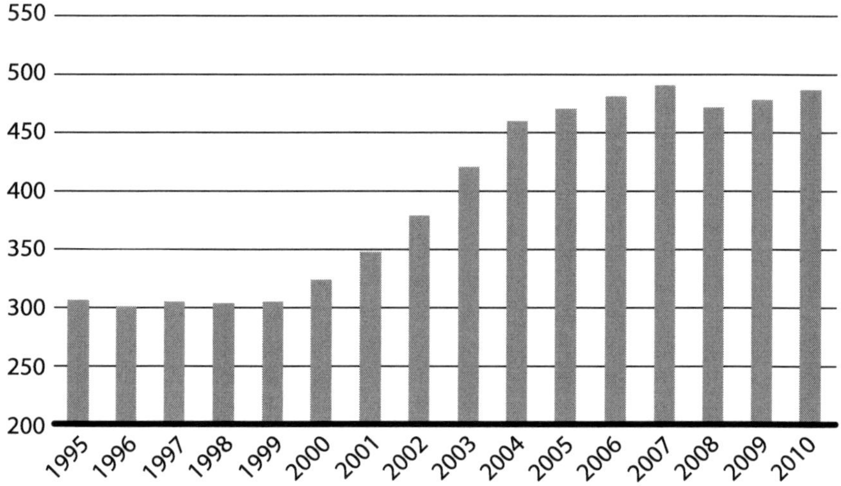

Figure 31. Oil production in Russia, 1995–2010 (millions of tons)
Sources: Goskomstat SSSR, Rosstat

The problem was not money. Money was a secondary issue both for the regime and for YUKOS. The real questions was who was more important in the country. Essentially, it was the repetition of a conflict that country had seen back in 1997. As we said earlier, the regime must not give up its legislative authority to business. But does that mean that in a confrontation the authorities should use selective prosecution and dubious legal methods? The regime's choice of those means raised harsh protest from the business community, political parties, and the public.[53]

After these actions, which included arrests, Berezovsky, Gusinsky, and other major entrepreneurs left the country. But the arrest of Khodorkovsky and the subsequent two trials still continue to arouse protest from the Russian and foreign public and a number of countries. The economic consequences, as well as the political ones, were dramatic: in 2006–7 a large portion of the oil industry was renationalized, after which oil production, which had been growing at a good clip after privatization, went down (Fig. 31).

* * *

The world economy of the last two centuries has been characterized by a combination of unprecedented acceleration of economic growth and economic cycles. After a period of five to ten years of robust economic growth, growth slows and sometimes is replaced by a decline in the major economies of the world. Much

53 www.newsru.com/Russia/25oct2003/rspp2.html.

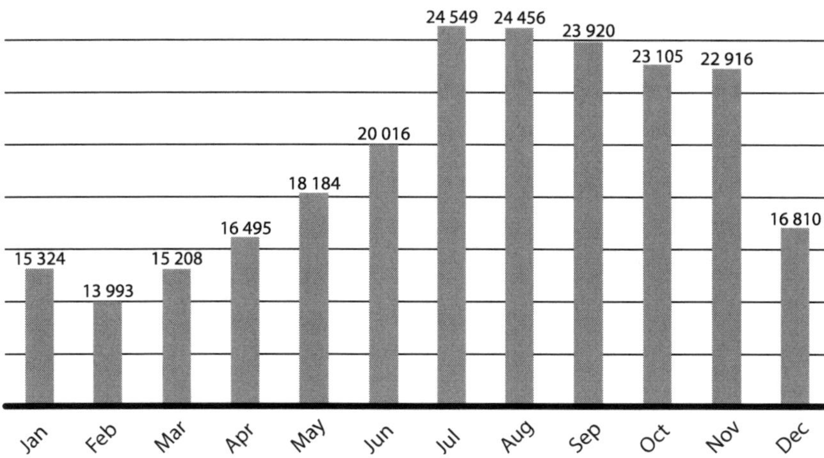

Figure 32. Gold currency reserves of Russia, 1997 (millions of dollars)
Source: Central Bank, Russian Federation

has been written about this manifestation, but as yet no one has learned how to predict economic crises. Macrostatistics that covered a long span of time revealed that the periods between the deepest declines in production have varied greatly and only in rare cases have been as long as nine to eleven years.[54]

For countries whose finances and balance of payments depend on the highly variable prices for raw materials, this creates risks. When there is a slowdown in global economic growth, there is a high probably of a worsening of the balance of payments and of a budget deficit. One more threat is a change in the direction of capital flow. Short-term investment comes to the markets of countries producing raw materials whose prices are at historical highs. But there is a quick outflow of investment when economic growth slows down and raw material prices fall. Hence the desire in countries dependent on market prices to protect against risks related to changes in global economic growth and changes in raw material prices.[55]

54 R. M. Entov, "Some Problems in Studying Business Cycles," Finansovyi krizis v Rossii i v mire," ed. Ye. T. Gaidar (Moscow: Prospekt, 2009), 6–39.

55 The Government Pension Fund (formerly the Government Petroleum Fund) was founded in Norway in 1990. On 1 January it became the Government Pension Fund—Global and the Government Pension Fund—Norway (formerly the National Insurance Scheme Fund). As of 20 June 2009 it had $395 billion (around 2.4 trillion Norwegian kroner), approximately 90 percent of GDP (estimate); in 2008, it had been more than $370 billion (approximately 2.1 trillion Norwegian kroner), or approximately 82 percent of GDP. Ministry of Finances of Norway, "The Government Pension Fund," www.regjeringen.no/en/dep/fin/Selected-topics/The-Government-Pension-Fund.html?id=1441; http://www.regjeringen.no/en/dep/fin/Selected-topics/The-Government-Pension-Fund.html?id=1441; article: http://www.ssb.no.

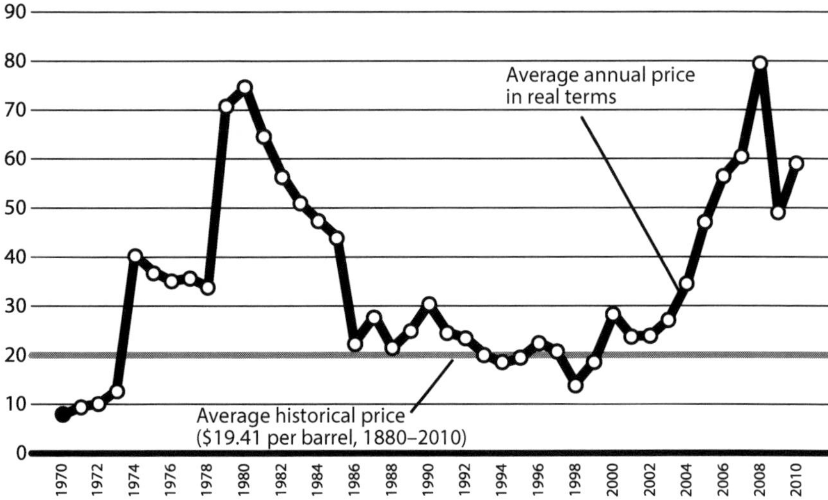

Figure 33. Crude oil price dynamics, 1970–2010 (in 2000 prices, dollars per barrel)
Sources: IMF, International Financial Statistics; WTRG Economics, http://wtrg.com

The drop in world oil prices in 1985–86 was not the cause of the collapse of the Soviet economy. The causes were deeper, related to the strategy of socialist industrialization chosen in the 1920s–1930s. However, the price drop was the trigger for the acute phase of the crisis. The Soviet Union had never established large currency reserves. It was difficult to talk about creating them in Russia in the 1990s. The country was getting back on its feet after a difficult crisis related to a collapse of the Soviet economy and had to service the foreign debt it inherited from the Soviet Union. In 1997 the gold currency reserves were growing gradually, but after the start of the crisis in Southeast Asia, they began to shrink again (Fig. 32).

The start of stable economic growth in 1999, the implementation of tax reform, and financial steadiness brought a question for the Russian authorities: create instruments that allow for the solving of financial problems when the market is not good for the most important raw materials, or spend the entire budget on current needs?

The discussion of this issue was fierce.[56] The Stabilization Fund of the Russian Federation was created on the basis of the law "On Amendments to the

56 See, for example, Postkommunisticheskaia Rossiia v kontekste mirovogo sotsial'no-ekonomicheskogo razvitiia, Nauchnye Trudy, no. 26 (Moscow: IEPP, 2001); S. Drobyshevskii, A. Zolotareva, P. Kadochnikov, and S. Sinel'nikov, Perspektivy sozdaniia stabilizatsionnogo fonda v RF, Nauchnye Trudy, no. 27 (Moscow: IEPP, 2001); E. Korop, Stabilizatsionnyi fond. Kakim on dolzhen byt'? Stabilizationnyi fond budet libo politicheskim, libo ego ne budet voobshche, 4 February 2003, www.finiz.ru.

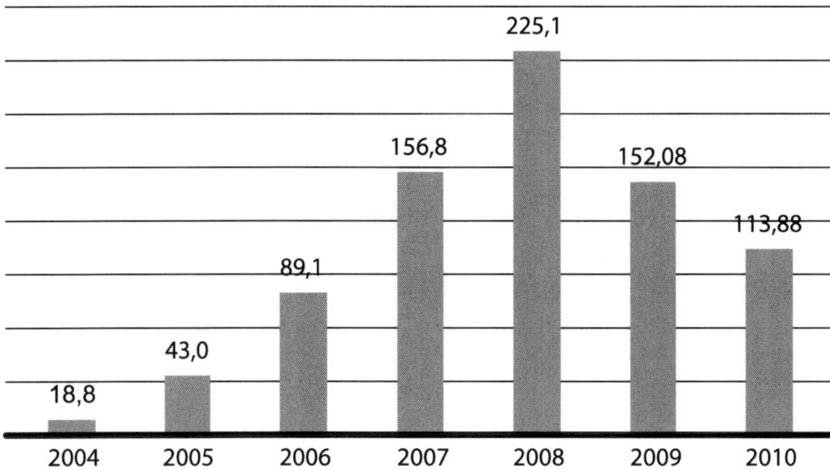

Figure 34. Size of the Stabilization Fund, 2004–7, and aggregate amount of the Reserve Fund and the National Welfare Fund, 2008 (billions of dollars)
Sources: Ministry of Finance; Central Bank, Russian Federation

Budget Code RF in Creating a Stabilization Fund RF," dated 23 December 2003 (no. 184-F3), which came into force on 1 January 2004. This happened before prices on the most important Russian exports reached a historically anomalous high (Fig. 33).

The arguments for creating the Stabilization Fund, later transformed into the Reserve Fund and the National Welfare Fund (Fig. 34), were that the country could not depend on factors that were hard to predict and which it could not control. The state had to have a financial reserve in order to manage the economic situation during a crisis in the markets.

Right up to 2007 the country's leadership supported a conservative policy promoted by the monetary and fiscal authorities. They believed that the growth rate of budget expenditures should not exceed the growth of the gross domestic product (Fig. 35). However, it is not easy to maintain this policy when there are anomalously high prices for exports. There were too many claims on the money in the Stabilization Fund. In 2006–7, when financial stabilization, a budget surplus, dynamic economic growth, and a fast increase in gold currency reserves (Fig. 36) accompanied by anomalously high oil prices became a reality, a new crossroads loomed.

Here is its essence: should the government continue the policy of accumulating income from exports and put it into liquid international assets, limiting the growth of budget expenditures, or should they give up this policy and start investing in the national economy at rates that exceeded GDP growth?

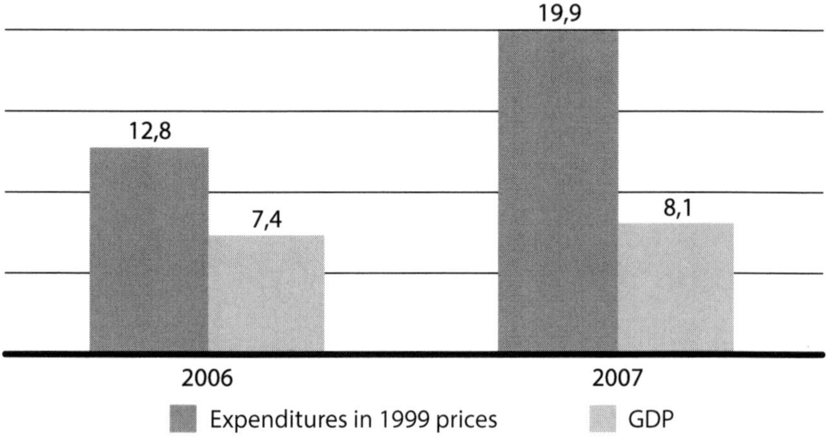

Figure 35. Rate of growth of expenditures of the expanded government of the Russian Federation and GDP, 2006–7, in real figures (percentage of previous year)
Sources: Rosstat, Roskazna

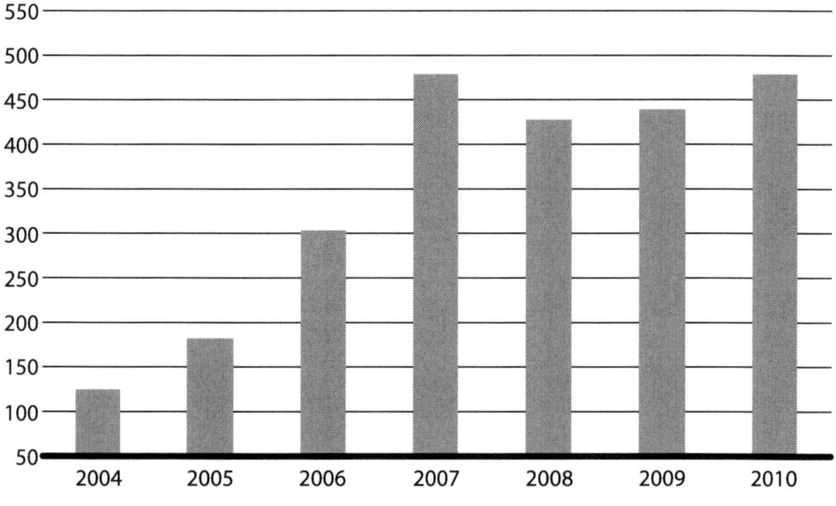

Figure 36. Gold currency reserves of Russia, 2004–10 (end of year, billions of dollars)
Source: Central Bank, Russian Federation

The decision was in favor of the latter.[57] The country's production powers are limited. They cannot be increased sharply over the course of just a few months. Therefore the increase in state spending in 2007 led only to increased inflation (Fig. 37). One of the channels connecting inflation rates with an overheated economy is a decrease in qualified workers (Fig. 38).

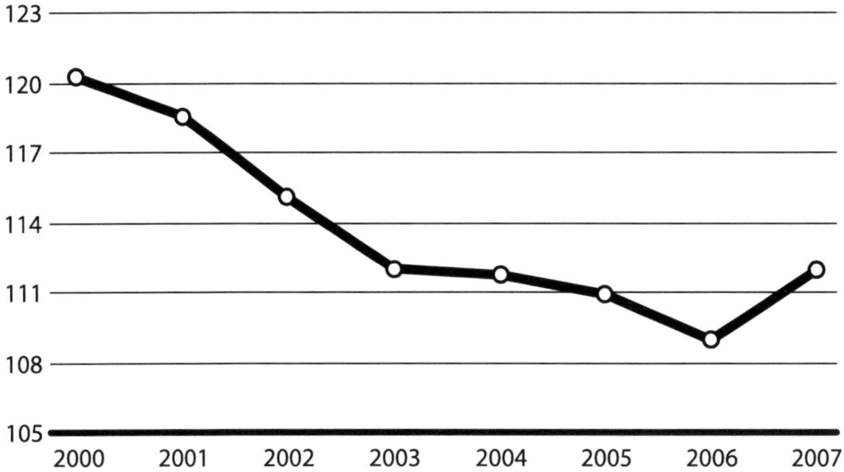

Figure 37. Inflation rates in Russia, 2000–7 (percentage of previous year)
Source: Rosstat

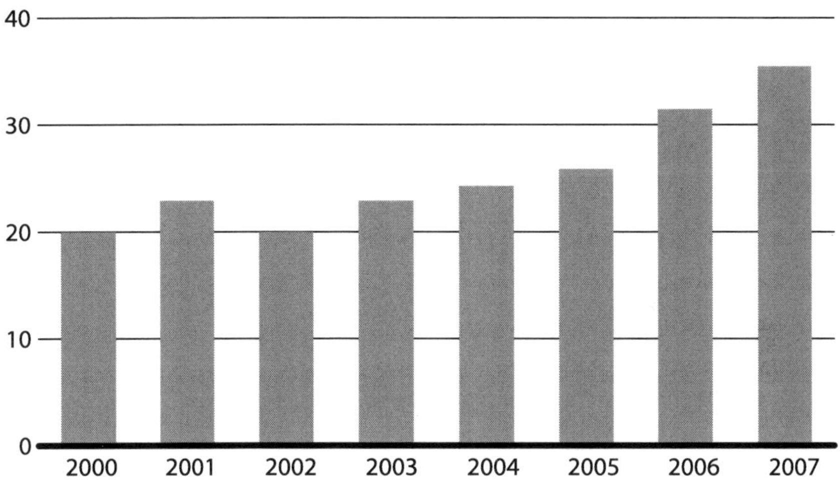

Figure 38. Percentage of industrial enterprises that considered a lack of workforce a hindrance to growth of production, 2000–7 (year average data)
Source: IET Surveys, www.iet.ru

57 S. Glazyev, "Report at a Meeting on Finding Ways of Using the Stabilization Fund," 16 June 2006, www.rodina.ru/article/show/?id=532; S. Glazyev, "The Stabilizaton Fund Is Phoney in Many Ways," www.rusk.ru/newsdata.php?idar=170221; E. Nikolaeva, "The Government and Ministry of Finance Did Not Defeat the Stabilization Fund," 26 February 2006, www.finiz.ru/economic/article989698; "Kopeikin Continues His Argument with Kudrin on the Stabilization Fund," March 2006, www.finiz.ru/ournews/article991599; E. Streltsov and E. Nikolaeva, "How to Spend the Stabilization Fund," 10 March 2006, www.finiz.ru/economic/article992831.

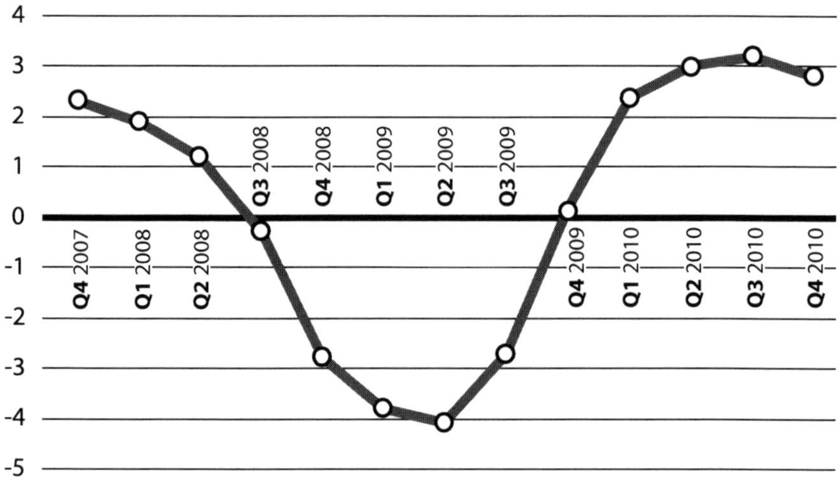

Figure 39. Rates of GDP growth in the United States in real terms, Q4 2007–Q4 2010 (percentage of corresponding period the previous year)
Source: U.S. Bureau of Economic Analysis, http://www.bea.gov

The attempt to accelerate economic growth beyond the level that the national economy could guarantee was made at an unfortunate moment. The world was moving toward a profound economic crisis. Few would argue with that now. And while the expert community cannot predict the time, causes, and scope of an economic crisis, it was not hard to guess that sooner or later global economic growth would slow down.

A significant number of Russian experts did not agree with the need to take into account the risks of a world economic slowdown for Russia's economic development.[58] Unfortunately, they were wrong. The crisis did unfold, and it struck our country hard. The U.S. Bureau of Economic Analysis, a highly authoritative organization that determines when the world's largest economy is in recession, declared in the fall of 2008 that the U.S. economy had been in recession since the end of 2007 (Figs. 39–42).

58 "There is no recession in the US and most likely by 2008 it won't happen. When Gaidar spoke of recession in January 2008, its likelihood was evaluated by the futures market at 80%. I then decided to express my disagreement with Gaidar's prediction and suggested that there probably would not be any recession at all. In the last six months, the recession has not come. Moreover, its probability today is evaluated much more modestly, at just 19%, which is one and half times less than in August of last year, when the mortgage crisis began; ... in July of last year oil prices were $70 a barrel, in July of this year, it's $140. For Russia, the world situation is inarguably much better than it was a year ago." A. Illarionov, "As a Liberal to a Nonliberal," 1 August 2008, www.izbrannoe.ru/43508.html.

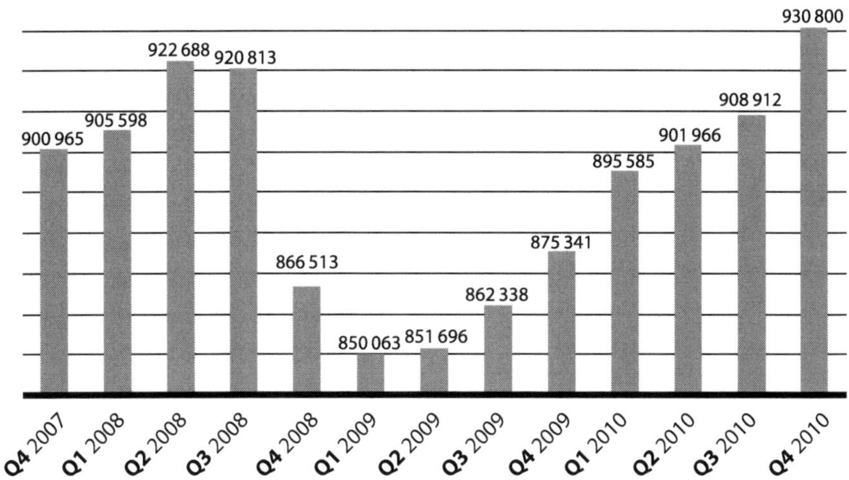

Figure 40. Volume of retail trade in the United States,* Q4 2007–Q4 2010 (millions of dollars)

* Seasonally adjusted

Source: Federal Reserve Bank of St. Louis, http://research.stlouisfed.org/fred2/series/RSFSXMV/downloaddata?cid=6

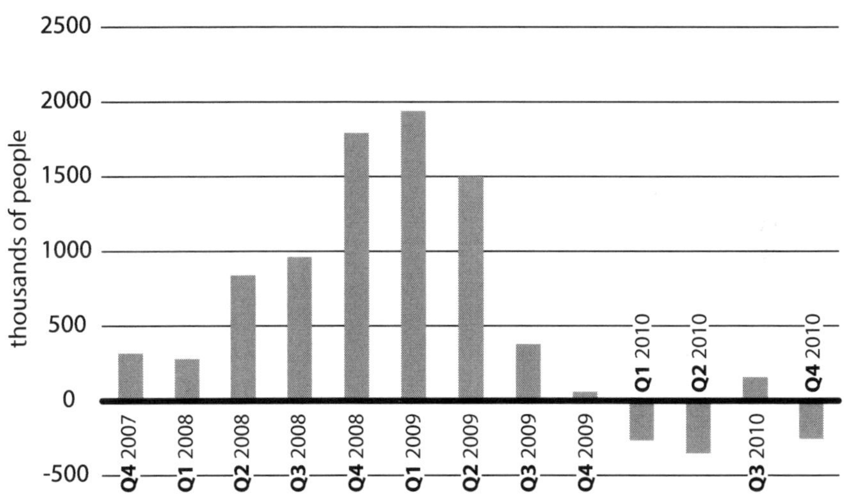

Figure 41. Residents of the United States* applying for unemployment benefits, Q4 2007–Q4 2010** (thousands of people)

* Seasonally adjusted

** Quarterly data based on published monthly data

Source: Federal Reserve Bank of St. Louis, http://research.stlouisfed.org/fred2/series/UNEMPLOY/download data?cid=12

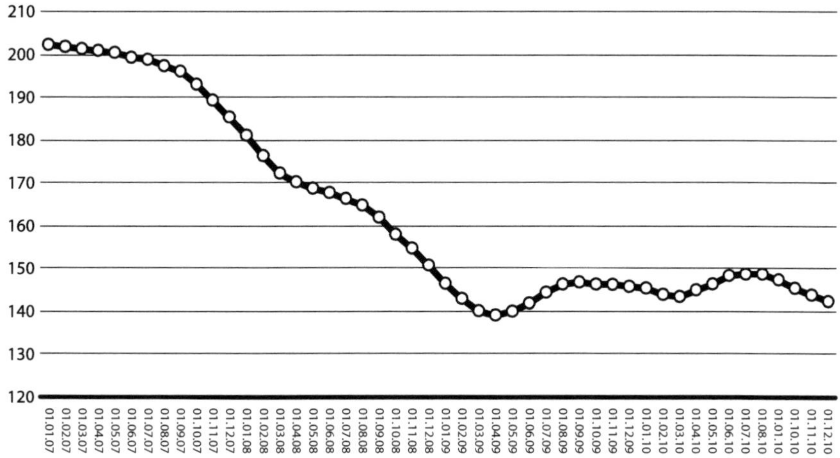

Figure 42. Real estate prices in the United States,* January 2007–December 2010 (percent)

* Case-Shiller Index (January 2000 = 100)

Source: Standard & Poor's, www2.standardandpoors.com/portal/site/sp/en/us/page.topic/indices_csmahp/2,3,4,0,0,0,0,0,0,0,0,0,0,0,0.html

Practice did not confirm the theory that India and China could guarantee stability in the world economy with slower or negative rates of economic growth in the US, Europe, and Japan (Table 13).

The decline in growth rates of the world economy affected raw material prices that were important for Russia (Fig. 43).

The change in oil prices came at a time of a radical change in the direction of capital flow (Fig. 44).

Table 13

IMF predictions for world economic growth for 2010, made in 2008–9; the estimate made in January 2010; and the actual number for 2010 (percentage of 2009 figure)

2008				2009				2010	
Apr	Jul	Oct	Nov	Jan	Apr	Jul	Sep	Jan (est.)	Actual
3.8	3.9	3.0	2.2	0.5	-1.3	-1.4	-1.1	-0.8	-0.6

Source: IMF, World Economic Outlook, April 2008–July 2009, www.imf.org

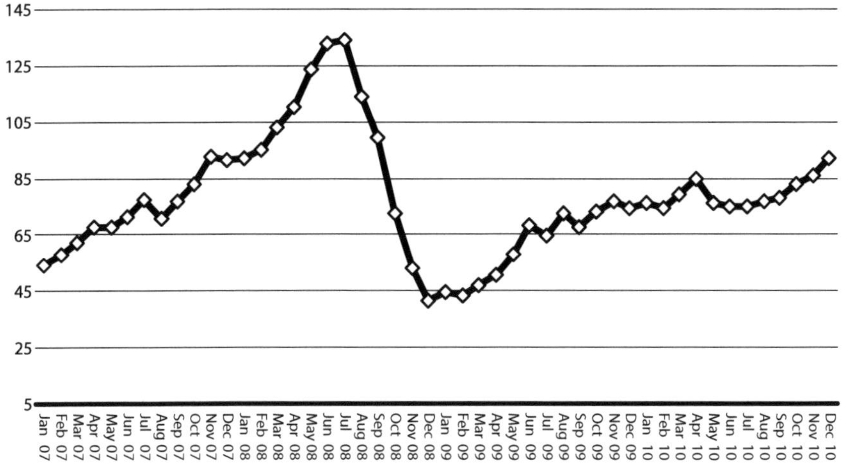

Figure 43. Prices for Brent oil, January 2007–December 2010 (dollars per barrel)
Source: IMF, International Financial Statistics database (CD-ROM), June 2009; Primary Commodity Prices database, www.imf.org/external/np/res/commod/index.asp

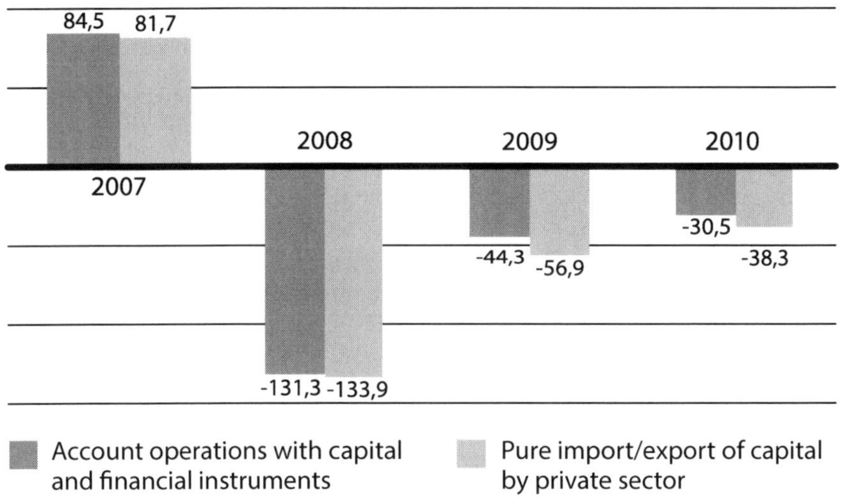

Figure 44. Inflow or outflow of capital from Russia, 2007–10 (billions of dollars)
Source: Central Bank, Russian Federation

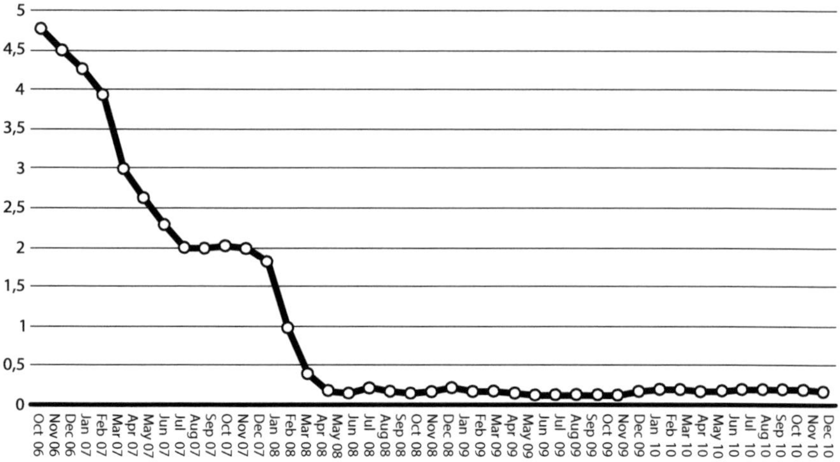

Figure 45. US federal funds rate, October 2007–December 2010 (percent)
Source: Federal Reserve, Statistical Release, www.federalreserve.gov/releases/h15/data.htm

Russia faced three interrelated challenges: a worsening of the balance of payments, a decrease in budget revenues, and an outflow of capital. But Russia was better prepared for these challenges than the Soviet Union had been. Russia's accumulated financial reserves and the flexibility of the exchange rate played their part.

Leaders of countries with world reserve currencies were forced to use financial expansion, increasing budget expenditures related to supporting the financial sector (Fig. 45).

In February 2008, the U.S. Congress and the Bush administration passed the first package of state measures, totaling $168 billion, to stimulate the U.S. economy. In early October, with the worsening of the financial crisis, Congress and the White House passed $700 billion worth of additional measures to stabilize financial markets.[59] In February 2009, the U.S. Senate approved a compromise stimulus plan proposed by the Obama administration, in the amount of $787 billion.[60]

The authorities in China did not legalize the market for capital operation in the national currency, but they began to discuss the possibility of this step. They understood that in this case the yuan would be one of the leading world reserve currencies. China chose the path of stimulating domestic demand.

---

59 www.rian.ru:80/us_news/20081124/155800218.html.

60 "An International Comparison of GDP in Europe in 1990," EEC UN, Geneva, 1994; "Lean Russia: Sustaining Economic Growth Through Improved Productivity," McKinsey, April 2009.

Figure 46. Exchange rate of Russian ruble and dollar (average for period), August 2008–December 2010 (rubles per dollar)
Source: Central Bank, Russian Federation

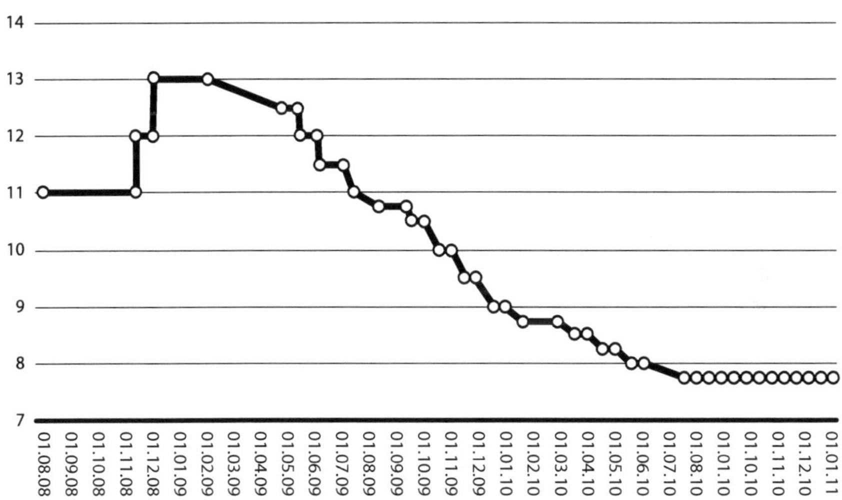

Figure 47. Interest on refinancing of Central Bank, Russian Federation, August 2008–January 2011 (percent)
Source: Central Bank, Russian Federation

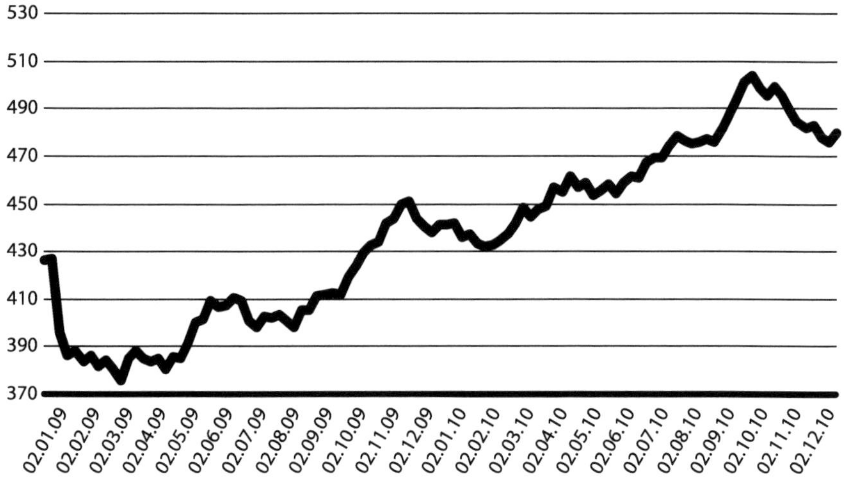

Figure 48. Gold currency reserves of Russia, 2009–10 (billions of dollars)
Source: Central Bank, Russian Federation

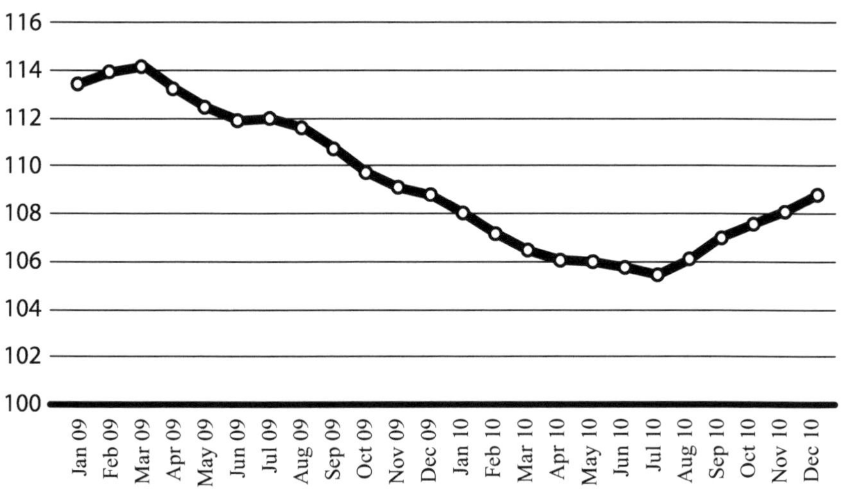

Figure 49. Inflation rates in Russia, January–December 2010 (percentage of corresponding period the previous year)
Source: Rosstat

The Russian authorities faced a new crossroads: stimulate demand, or concentrate on preserving financial stability and steadiness of the banking system?

Their position was asymmetrical but reasonable. The ruble is not a leading world reserve currency and will not become one in the near future. The Russian fiscal and monetary authorities decided that starting in autumn 2008 the main priorities would be preserving financial stability and the banking system, adapting the economy to new conditions, and preserving hard currency reserves. The result of this choice was a lowering of the exchange rate of the ruble with regard to the basic reserve currencies (Fig. 46) and a raising of the base interest rate of the Central Bank (Fig. 47). The Central Bank's interest rate did not change until January 2009, when the gold currency reserves stopped diminishing (Fig. 48).

These measures made it possible to stabilize the exchange rate and break the trend of rising inflation (Fig. 49). Note: from 1 to 7 September 2009, the index of consumer prices, according to Rosstat, was 100.0 percent, at the start of the month, 100.0, at the start of the year, 108.1 percent; in 2008, from the start of the month, 100.1 percent, from the start of the year, 109.8 percent, and as a whole for September, 100.8 percent.

An acute banking crisis was averted. But the decisions taken were not simple. Their first result was a harsh change in productivity, shifting from vibrant economic growth to a decline (Figs. 50–52, Table 14). The second result was a radical worsening in the labor market (Fig. 53).

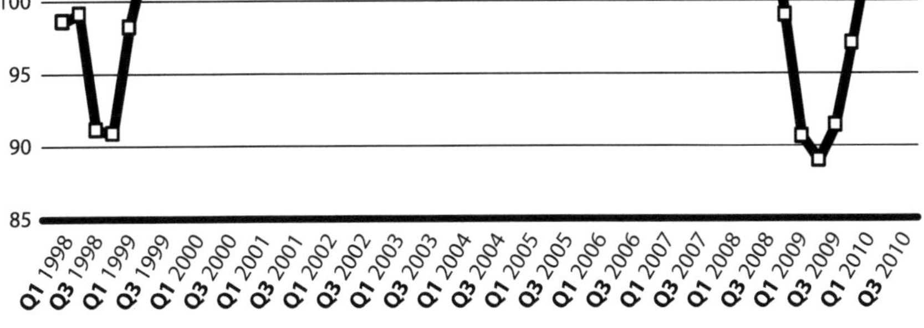

Figure 50. Russia's GDP in real terms, Q1 1998–Q3 2010 (percentage of corresponding period the previous year)

Sources: Rosstat; database, SU-HSE, http://stat.hse.ru/exes/tables/GDP_Q_I.htm

Figure 51. Index of industrial production, Q1 1998–Q4 2009 (percentage of corresponding period the previous year)

Sources: Rosstat; database, SU-HSE, http://stat.hse.ru/exes/tables/IND_Q_I.htm

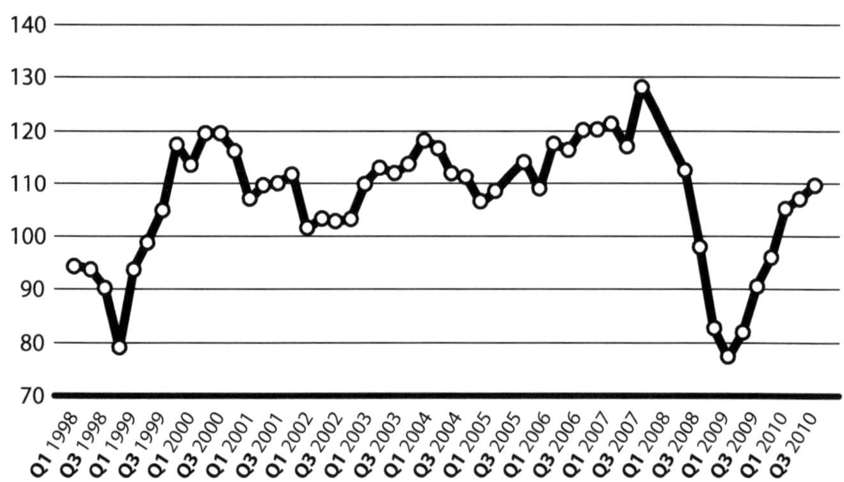

Figure 52. Investments in basic capital, Q1 1998–Q4 2010* (percentage of corresponding period the previous year)

* Estimate

Sources: Rosstat; database, SU-HSE, http://stat.hse.ru/exes/tables/INVFC_Q_I.htm

Table 14

Balance of expanded government of Russian Federation budget, Q1 2008 to Q4 2010 (percentage of GDP)

	I	II	III	IV
2008	11.2	10.0	12.2	-13.3
2009	2.7	-8.6	-3.5	-13.6
2010	2.5	0.3	-1.4	-14.0

Sources: Roskazna; Rosstat; Economic Expert Group, www.eeg.ru

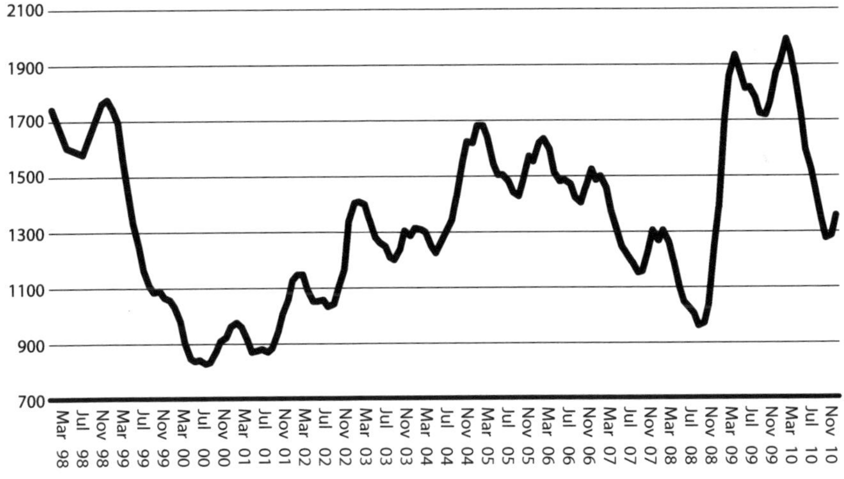

Figure 53. Number of people receiving unemployment benefits, March 1998–December 2010 (end of month, thousands of people)
Data for 1998: number of people eligible for unemployment insurance

Sources: Rosstat, Obzor eknomiki Rossii. Osnovnye tendentsii razvitia. 1998.III (translated from English) (Moscow: Russian-European Center of Economic Policy, 1998), www.budgetrf.ru/Publications/Magazines/recep/1998/4/rcpb199840000work/rcpb199840000work010.htm

Crossroads of Our Times

Today Russian authorities face three key crossroads.[61] Unlike all the others analyzed previously, they deal with Russia's future, not the past, and they cannot be considered as behind us yet. The choice in each case will have a profound strategic influence on our country's fate in the coming decades.

The first is this: Can we agree that the worst is behind us, reject a conservative budgetary and monetary policy, and concentrate our efforts on developing the real sector? Or must we retain the previous monetary and credit policy and the economic and political priorities chosen in fall 2008?

It is our opinion that rejecting a conservative budgetary and monetary policy would be irresponsible and dangerous.

It is hard today to predict how the global crisis will develop and how it will affect Russia. The measures taken by the United States, the leading members of the European Union, Japan, and China can mitigate for a few months the effects of the crisis on the global economy. However, it is hard to say whether these efforts will produce stable results. The scale of the problems in the banking systems of the leading European countries is not clear. Nor is it easy to understand how the difficulties involved in paying corporate obligations will be handled in the first six months of 2010. No one knows how likely it is that a crisis on the "bubble" model will develop in China. If you don't know how the crisis will develop, you have to go on the worst-case scenario. Russia, which has the experience of a currency catastrophe that led to the collapse of the Soviet Union, has to be particularly careful.

The second crossroads: will we be able to build an innovative economy and get in line with competitive highly developed states, or will Russia gradually find itself in the group of poorly developed nations? Essentially this crossroads appears today in a very clear form: innovation or degradation?

What is the historical background for this choice?

For all the inefficiency of the Soviet economy, it created unique technological achievements in atomic science and space exploration. All, without exaggeration, belong among the greatest scientific and technological achievements of the twentieth century. Yet neither then nor later was the Soviet economy capable of creating high-quality consumer technology. Soviet cars, televisions, radios, and other consumer goods almost always yielded in quality to foreign merchandise.

---

61 Editor's note: This text was written by Yegor Gaidar in November–December 2009.

The successes and the failure of Soviet innovation were determined by the base qualities of the Soviet economy. Totally state-focused, it could create demand only when and where the state developed a great need. It was almost always related to the global geopolitical confrontation and projects in the defense sphere. At the same time, monetary demand coming from the public could not be a signal for the Soviet economy, for by its nature such demand could not be perceived by the centralized planned economy. In that sense, as world scientific and technological progress developed, the backwardness of the Soviet economy became more obvious.

In the early 1970s, Soviet science entered a period of slower development, followed by stagnation. Despite promising individual results, the Soviet research institutes were turning into a symbol of the inefficient use of the country's intellectual potential.

It was no accident that Mikhail Gorbachev's first initiative after his election as general secretary of the Central Committee of the Communist Party was formulated as a conception of accelerating scientific and technological progress, and the Central Committee held hearings on that subject in June 1985, with the keynote address given by Gorbachev himself.[62] The party elite sensed that the Soviet economy was not responding to innovations and that something had to be done. Various programs were elaborated, but all attempts to solve this problem failed.

In the next twenty years, under conditions of market transformations and an open economy, some industries degraded, reducing output of means of transportation, factory equipment, textile equipment, sewn goods, and so on. However, other industries developed well, for example the production of electrical equipment, metallurgy, chemistry, petrochemicals, telecommunications, and high-rise construction. The aggregated index of industrial production in Russia in 2008 was on the level of the early 1990s (Fig. 54).

Labor productivity in Russia, in terms of purchasing power parity, practically did not change between 1990 and 2007, remaining around 30 percent of that in the United States.

During that period, there was a structural reconfiguration of the economy, which allowed the country to maintain the level of general economic development, but did not give an impetus to innovation. According to GU-HSE, the share of enterprises introducing innovations in Russia is no higher than 10–11 percent, while in the developed countries of the European Union the share is 70 percent and in less developed countries of the European Union it is 20–25 percent.[63]

---

62 http://postsov.rsux.ru/chronicl/1985/11_06.shtml.

63 Ya. Kuzminov, "Growth of the RF Economy in the Crisis Depends on Innovations," RIA Novosti, 12 November 2008, www.rian.ru/crisis_news/20081112/154880151.html.

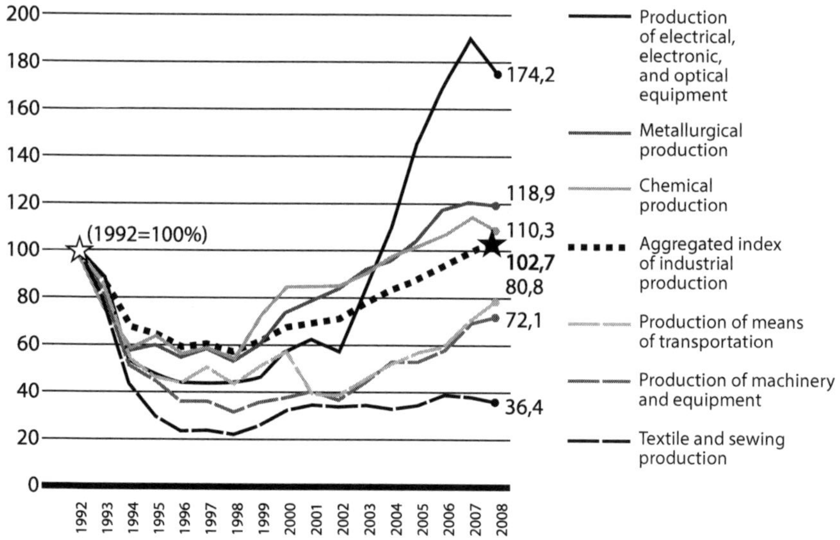

Figure 54. Growth of production by industry
Source: Rosstat, www.rusnano.com

According to data from the 2008–9 World Economic Forum, Russia ranked 51st out of 134 countries in global competitiveness and in 48th place for innovation activity.[64] Thus, the serious gap between our country and world leaders, first noted in the mid-1970s, has still not been narrowed.

The phenomenon of successful innovation models for countries took root in the last twenty years, while Russia was focused on the historic task of building a market economy and starting economic growth. The United States was among the first to create the innovation model for developing the economy, in the early 1960s, and it managed to establish it by the 1980s. Taiwan, one of the leaders in the innovation world, needed twenty-five years; Israel and South Korea took twenty. In the early 1990s the Finnish economy was in a catastrophic state because of the collapse of the USSR and the loss of Finland's role as the Soviet "window" on Europe. However, today Finland, which previously had almost no high-tech industries, is one of the leaders of the innovation economy.

In the 2000s, Russia's economic growth was driven by raw materials, with their well-known limitations. Without setting ourselves the task of a serious analysis in this work, we will note that a number of countries embarked on building an innovation economy with a substantially lower level of develop-

64 World Economic Forum, The Global Competitiveness Report 2008–2009, 289, https://members.weforum.org/pdf/GCR08/GCR08.pdf.

ment in these spheres than contemporary Russia (for example, South Korea or Taiwan in the early 1990s). It should also be noted that in the last five to seven years these areas have received significant state support in Russia. Many higher schools, among them some in the provinces, have world-class research equipment. Despite the problems that remain, these schools have been given an impetus for both education and research. Very highly qualified people with a high level of technological and engineering skills work in Russia's manufacturing and industries of the "new economy," including the atomic industry, aviation and space, power mechanical engineering, and telecommunications. Thus, the starting conditions for expansion of innovation in these fields are no worse than they were in many countries that managed to do it.

There has been a lot of discussion of late about the roles of the state and of private business in building an innovation economy. It seems to us that it would be a mistake to take an extreme position here. In elaborating the Russian situation in this regard, we must look closely at world experience and the real state of these institutions in our country.

It is hardly necessary to say that the movement toward an innovation economy must be built on such market values as private property, competition, universally accepted rules of the game, long-term macroeconomic stability, and low inflation. There isn't a single country that has been successful at innovation that proves otherwise.

Yet the role of the state in promoting the innovation process is extremely important. In Israel, the state program Yozma created the venture capital industry. The state contributed more than $100 million. The Office of the Chief Scientist, a division of the Ministry of Industry, Trade, and Labor, operates there with an annual budget of around $500 million. In South Korea state expenditures supporting innovation in private business total $1 billion. Finland gives 582 million euros to its TEKES and SITRA programs. The U.S. government gives up to $2 billion a year to the Small Business Innovation Research program.

Every country develops its own innovation model. In Israel the greater part of the innovation economy ends with the establishment and subsequent sale of rights to new intellectual property; there are almost no major companies there producing high-tech products. In Japan and South Korea, on the contrary, there are few small innovation businesses. In some countries fundamental research is weak, but there is an innovation economy oriented toward new technologies. In selecting the aims and priorities of innovation policy, the state must base its decision on real factors such as existing stock and domestic and world demand. Russia has yet to find its model, but obviously one of its most important components will be the balance between the roles of business and the regime in investing in the country's innovation development.

Serious investment in innovation development by business cannot be expected if the necessary legal climate is not in place. The first steps have been taken in Russia to put in place legislation that will stimulate an innovation economy. However, the scale of the tasks that remain to be done in this sphere will require several years of consistent work. We will list only the most important areas of legislation needing changes, if not serious reworking.

The present corporate law is not commensurate with the needs of a developing innovation economy. It lacks modern organizational and legal forms for actually doing innovation. Limited-liability companies, joint-stock companies, and partnerships do not give flexible maneuverability to capital or create agreements that legally bind not only shareholders but also management and sometimes even potential consumers. Without such flexibility, many start-ups would be impossible to launch. We also lack adequate ways to form venture capital funds, familiar to the world innovation community. The form proposed by our legislation, closed privatization investment funds, is cumbersome and overregulated, since it was not created for this aim but was just an attempt to adjust for use in innovation projects an instrument that was created to attract money from small investors.

The tax laws need to be changed as well. In recent years, the focus was on plugging tax loopholes, and there was an almost total absence of stimulus mechanisms. Today we need much more complex constructions to stimulate innovation activity and the export of high-tech products. The amendments passed at the end of 2010 doing away with taxation of capital gains are correct, but this is just one of many needed reforms.

Customs laws need to be reexamined as well. As far as the customs agency is concerned, the export of a million tons of grain and the export of biochips with a sample of organic material are the same. With export rules like this, it is impossible to interact with the world of innovation.

The time has come for radical changes in technical regulation. We must admit that the present law on technical regulation does not work. There are still remnants of the Soviet system in rules passed in recently that mix milk standards with five unrelated things. We can continue living this way if our economic growth remains tied to oil exports. We cannot work this way if our goal is to build an innovation economy.

Today, the rights to the results of research and development carried out with co-financing from the state budget belong to the state. Chapter 4 of the Civil Code permits transferring them to the citizens who created those new technologies and products, but the bureaucratic reality excludes that possibility. We believe that what is needed here is to make it obligatory for the state to turn over this intellectual property, rather than simply giving permission for the state to do it. Currently this intellectual property continues to belong to the state, that is, to no one. The only possibility of acquiring the right to it involves a juridical person executing a state contract. Most often, that juridical person is an organization funded by the state budget. The lack of stimulus, motivation, and entrepreneurial activity of these ineffective owners is well known. In order to encourage innovation based on scientific and engineering research, we essentially need to privatize intellectual property—we need an "intellectual amnesty."

Immigration law needs amendment, too. The first steps in its liberalization, taken in 2010, are positive. However, we need a deeper rethinking of its conceptual direction. While we must have limits on unskilled labor, we need to encourage highly skilled labor. Without this, we cannot modernize the economy.

The ways of developing the infrastructure needed for an innovation economy need profound reexamination. This applies to the financial infrastructure (grants, seed money, pre-seed money, and venture capital) as well as to non-financial elements (technology parks, business incubators, technology transfer centers, and technology innovation zones). Infrastructure cannot be created without the state. According to the statistics, there are thousands of technology parks, business incubators, and technology transfer centers in Russia—they are all on the books. But very few of them exist in real life. Often they are simply not what they are said to be. The conditions in which these organizations work are not commensurate with their goals. That means the normative base and control systems are unacceptable. Yet building an innovation economy without the appropriate infrastructure is impossible.

We believe that innovation should be mandatory for large (and especially monopolist) state companies. The state has matured enough to demand activity in this sphere from them. The idea of implementing innovation programs similar to investment ones is reasonable. The investment programs that were put in place developed methodology, organizational procedures, and structural subdivisions over a period of five to ten years. Now the step must be taken from investments to innovations, from growth to changing the quality of growth. Innovation programs with clear goals, budgets, and deadlines must be created within large state companies. For example, petroleum companies must find ways to extract more oil from existing strata; energy producers might focus on increasing the efficiency of generation or lowering losses in the networks. Full programs, suitable for supervision, must be developed for these goals.

This approach does not work with private business. If a private company does something major in the innovation sphere, it is within its rights to expect support from the state. In recent years almost every large private company applied for help from the state; therefore, that aid should be conditional on the implementation of innovation. Business will understand that kind of logic.

Regional innovation policy is extremely important. It is not possible to have the right conditions for innovations everywhere, and the creation of a complete innovation ecosystem is a subtle and hard-to-control process, in which financial and organizational conditions are no less important than the regional environment and atmosphere. In the United States, half of the entire high-tech innovation economy is located in just two states: California and Massachusetts. In

Russia, Tomsk and Kazan have taken the lead in the innovation economy. They have dozens of high-class innovation companies with a volume of hundreds of millions of dollars. Their experience must be studied and promoted.

Serious transformations in the structure and function of federal agencies of the executive branch will be required. As we see it, there should be one ministry that concentrates on innovation policy. The most natural approach would be add to the powers of the Ministry of Economic Development, turning it into something like a Ministry of Economics and Innovation Policy, rather than creating a new unit. Additionally, almost every other ministry should have a deputy in charge of subdivisions dealing with innovation. The state must solve this organizational management issue.

Thus, implementation of an innovation economy will require a complex of efforts by the state and business in a wide variety of areas. This will have to be undertaken despite the handicap of a weak culture of private property and little protection for it. It will have to deal with extensive corruption, an ineffective court system, weak competition in most industries and a complete lack of competition in the political system, and state control over the leading electronic media. But this does not mean that the country cannot and should not be set on the track toward innovation development.

The paradox lies in the fact that despite these conditions, the innovation economy exists in many regions. In the last ten to fifteen years, Danaflex in Kazan, Mikran in Tomsk, Monokristall in Stavropol, Novomet in Perm, and many other enterprises that started from scratch are working at world-class innovation levels today. Many of them have a significant share of exports, a sales volume over $100 million, and growth of 20–40 percent annually. They appeared when the state did not have a goal of developing the innovation economy and in fact was erecting barriers to hold it back. Yet these companies achieved success.

We must realize that we need innovation most of all. Manufacturers in other countries are ready to sell Russia everything. New Airbus and Boeing jets are being sold to us, and planes from Bombadier are coming up, so our Sukhoi jets are needed for the development of Russia.

However considerable the tasks of innovation policy may be for the state, we must understand that the main driver of innovation development in Russia can only be private business. The state can and must formulate the goals and priorities of innovation policy, create conditions, stimulate, and promote, but the actual creation of a commercial innovation product will always be the prerogative of private business. In Russia, this kind of business is very young. Just two decades ago, private entrepreneurship was punishable by three to eight years in prison. Since then, Russian business moved out of kiosks and into modern retail and wholesale chains with the latest technology. It has mastered medium, large, and major industrial production. In a number of industries our businessmen compete with global companies. Russian business has traveled the path from "grannies selling socks" under the presidential decree "On Freedom of Trade" in 1992 to major private transnational companies in modern manufacturing. The creation of a new quality—the innovation economy—is the main challenge facing Russian private business today.

This does not mean that we should not modernize the political system. The mistake is in the artificial division between political and economic modernization. Logical constructs along the lines of "Let's wait until they create a democratic political system for us and then we'll start creating an innovation economy" are totally unacceptable. If the country had developed in accordance with this logic, it would still not have private property or a market economy.

Therefore, in order to build an innovation economy in Russia, the quality of governance must be improved substantially, and at the same time private business must offer a powerful positive push. These two important institutions must take up this new historical task and rebuild their mutual interaction. In terms of complexity, this reform is comparable to the transformations our country lived through in the last twenty years. It is unlikely to be harder. For all their problems, neither the political nor the economic system in contemporary Russia can keep us from responding positively to this challenge.

The crossroads at which we must choose between degradation or innovation will have to be put behind us, and a full-fledged innovation economy must be built in the time frame given to us by history—approximately fifteen to twenty years.

The third crossroads confronting the Russian authorities today has an economic basis, but the decision on which path to take bears a political character. Russia's ruling elite came to power during the nascent restorative growth, when the basic institutions of the market economy were formed and the society adapted, albeit with difficulty, to the new reality. Then came ten years of dynamic growth in GDP and in real income of the population. From 2004, economic growth was supported by the expansion of budget maneuverability tied to rising oil prices (Fig. 55).

Under these conditions, preserving the stability of the political regime is not difficult. You would have to try very hard to be an unpopular leader when real income goes up 10 percent annually for ten years. But today's situation, when the real income has stopped growing and is going down (Fig. 56), is radically different.

For those who run a country whose budget revenues depend on raw materials markets, this is a new and difficult crossroads: the choice is either a tightening of political control, with repressions against those who do not agree and control over small media, or the reestablishment of the system of checks and balances, freedom of the press, and real federalism.

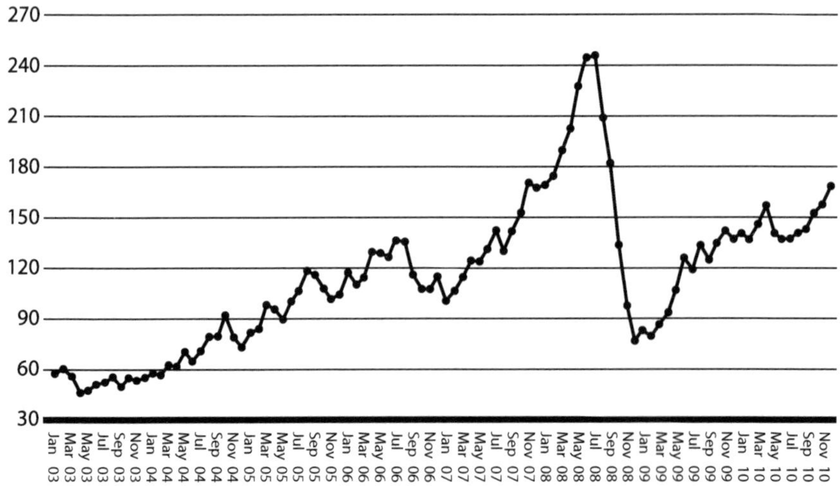

Figure 55. Prices for Brent oil in real terms,* January 2003—December 2010 (index; 2005 = 100)
Source: IMF

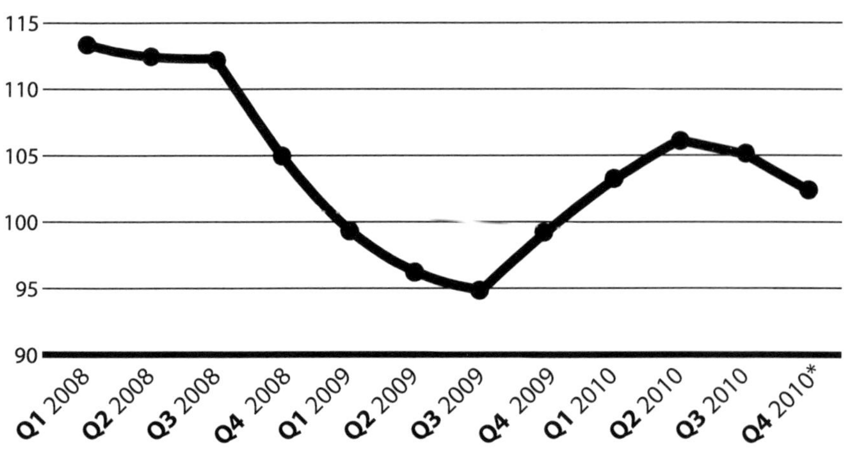

Figure 56: Real income, Q1 2008–Q4 2010 (percentage of corresponding period the previous year)
* Preliminary data
Source: Rosstat, www.gks.ru/bgd/regl/B09_02/Main.htm

The first path leads to a new revolution. The two revolutions our country went through in the twentieth century seem more than enough. We are not the first country to have to make this decision. When Western Europe gradually chose this path, unprecedented economic growth began. We hope that the Russian authorities facing this crossroads will make the right choice.